Creative mathematics

The teaching and learning of school mathematics has always been problematic. Particularly in primary and middle schools, tensions abound concerning understanding, processes and 'application' of mathematics in relation to explorations of genuine, 'authentic' contexts.

This book offers detailed accounts of seven- to ten-year-old pupils engaging in extensive projects that integrate mathematics with the visual and musical arts. These projects occurred in the children's normal classroom for one afternoon per week over the course of most of a school year, and resulted in significant products. For the pupils, the things they made were both a source of delight and a means to see the aesthetic power of mathematics in action. For the teacher, these objects additionally offered the opportunity for non-traditional mathematics assessment.

The authors' voices, those of a researcher, a schoolteacher and a university lecturer, combine to produce an engaging and unusual narrative which will prove inspiring both to trainee and practising primary/middle school teachers, as well as to mathematics educators.

Rena Upitis is Dean of the Faculty of Education, Queen's University, Kingston, Canada. **Eileen Phillips** is an elementary school teacher in Vancouver, British Columbia. **William Higginson** is Co-ordinator of the Mathematics, Science and Technology Education Group at Queen's University.

Creative mathematics

Exploring children's understanding

Rena Upitis, Eileen Phillips
and William Higginson

London and New York

First published 1997
by Routledge
11 New Fetter Lane, London EC4P 4EE

Simultaneously published in the USA and Canada
by Routledge
29 West 35th Street, New York, NY 10001

Typeset in Garamond by Solidus (Bristol) Limited
Printed and bound in Great Britain by
Biddles Ltd, Guildford and King's Lynn

British Library Cataloging in Publication Data
A catalogue record for this book is available from the British Library

Library of Congress Cataloguing in Publication Data
A catalogue record for this book has been requested

ISBN 0-415-16462-1 (hbk)
ISBN 0-415-16463-x (pbk)

Contents

Figures

Preface
Encounters with the real

This is a book about teaching and learning and mathematics. It is also about the boundaries, tensions and connections between these activities. It is a book about children in schools; about teachers, researchers and mathematicians – and about the boundaries, tensions and connections among these roles. It is about actions, ideas, and things – and about utility, beauty, and products of mathematics.

Mathematics has always had a troubled involvement with objects in the material world. This book deals explicitly with objects and their creation. The authors show how the children successfully made things, with mathematical ideas as one of the components. In so doing, the children also furthered their understanding of mathematics itself.

Creative mathematics presents a voice trio (with a Greek-style chorus of children's voices in accompaniment). Each voice is present in its own section in every chapter, though the voice-leading varies as the book unfolds. It tells a lively and thought-provoking story of a year-long encounter when one teacher-researcher (Rena) worked for an afternoon a week in the third- and fourth-grade classroom (children 7–10 years in age) of another (Eileen). Rena and Eileen describe and think aloud about the large-scale mathematical challenges they offered these pupils, as well as the challenges they themselves encountered in so doing. It is about the presence of an outsider soon to become an insider in a vibrant classroom, and the perturbations and possibilities that this additional presence generated.

We are also offered a third voice (Bill's), one from further afield, both in space and time, whose after-the-fact reflections take us further afield too. Bill brings us into the world of mathematicians writing about ideas, and how the increasing availability of technology can facilitate access to them.

Many of the projects the children worked on may not, at first glance, seem particularly 'mathematical' in nature: but extensive 'mathematicking' did, in fact, take place. The tellers recount and identify elements of mathematical activity, mathematical thinking, and mathematical presence manifest in the pupils' work. The trio also provide evidence of ways in which the classroom atmosphere and dynamics supported the children's creative powers, as well as enriched their intellectual and emotional lives in some striking and inspiring ways.

The book begins with a two-plus-one structure at work among the three authors. It begins with Rena and Bill, in the same place in Kingston, Ontario where they both work as university-based teacher educators, discussing Rena's forthcoming sabbatical year in Vancouver, British Columbia (some two thousand plus miles away). They talked of the exploratory work Rena wanted to carry out in the classroom of an as-yet-unknown other.

The enterprise was not originally conceived as a fully collaborative venture with a particular teacher. Rena, the 'outsider', was simply hoping to be allowed to work on her own with some of this teacher's pupils on projects of her own devising. But very quickly after arriving in Eileen's classroom, it became clear that Rena and she were well able to work together in the same classroom space, with boundaries between outsider and insider soon rendered porous. At this stage, it was Bill who became the 'plus one' in relation to Rena and Eileen being the 'two'. So one additional area of interest to readers could be how someone might work successfully alongside a teacher in their classroom.

I mentioned the word 'tensions' earlier. Tensions are not necessarily negative: they can highlight the seams between things that often remain unseen, and can be used productively (as in ropes and sails, for example). Some of what Eileen writes about is what she saw; some of what Rena tells about is what she did. But as the book develops, as their relationship develops and changes, these separate positions (including teacher, learner, recipient, observer, researcher, insider, outsider) blend and merge, and both joint planning and joint doing occur. We learn significant things about how to be with young children in a mathematical way.

Among the tensions acknowledged and explored are the following.

- *Issues of status, expertise and authority*

For instance, Eileen's initial unease and trepidation included the prospect of having a university teacher educator, one she saw as 'an expert', in her classroom. On the one hand, she wondered whether Rena might find her lacking in certain ways or engaging in *démodé* classroom practices (despite feeling she presented a strong mathematics curriculum), while at the same time not wanting to be 'told' how to teach mathematics by someone without anything like her twenty-five years of classroom experience. How much extra work might this enterprise entail? What if the experience turned into a nightmare, and she had committed herself to an entire year of it?

- *How teachers make decisions about mathematical areas into which they are not willing to venture*

One example of this is Rena's decision to back away from exploring tessellating pentagons, despite Bill seeing her as able to contend with uncertainty and not-knowing in any setting. Another example is Eileen's backing away from plane symmetry, because at the time she could not see the difference between line and plane symmetry.

- *Coping with the prevailing mathematical culture of school and beyond*

This is illustrated by Eileen's encounters with some parents' expectations of mathematics, and by Bill's reflections on pre-service teachers' expectations and perceived needs.

- *Engaging with controversy surrounding the nature of 'legitimate' accounts of classroom exploration*

For instance, in this book, the conventional apparatus of research reporting, such as identifying explicit research questions, presenting lengthy transcripts of audio- and videotaped records, and making systematic and prolific reference to the published literature, is deliberately eschewed in favour of a more immediate and engaging reporting style.

- *Classroom dynamics*

For instance, Eileen talks of deciding to push a project through: she reports time pressures, concerned that there might not be enough time to do a good job. She also mentions noise pressures, wondering if the productive engagement in one part of the class might be disturbing the work of another. Finally, she relates how she created the time for herself to work at one of these project tasks alongside her pupils: a simple but profound classroom issue of struggling herself to embody 'doing as I ask you to do'.

- *General issues of coping with planning and organising activity with two adults, each with different responsibilities (initially, Eileen was responsible for the class, Rena for suggesting projects)*

For example, we read how Rena and Eileen came to plan aloud in the class sessions – for a discussion of some values of this practice, see Chapter 3 of Jackson (1992). Also, Eileen talks about her feeling of being on the sidelines in the animation project, frustrated because she was very interested in what was going on in the other part of the room while being involved herself in working with her own group.

In addition to these particular tensions, there are sub-texts that run throughout. The authors write about their deliberations over choice of labels to describe themselves: for example, 'teacher', 'researcher', 'mathematician'. Who has the right to use these? In response, the authors reveal to us a substantial amount of their personal mathematical history, both as learners and teachers. This is an important discussion, for it helps situate not only the writers but also the significance of their work.

Another important sub-text that runs throughout the book is that of deepening connections and developing relationships:

- of these three adults to each other, and with us as readers, as they recount and reveal aspects of their own varied relationships to mathematics;
- of aspects of teaching to aspects of learning, for adults and children alike;
- of offered task to actual activity when observed from a mathematical frame.

A third sub-text I observed was that of a concern with the 'real'. 'Genuine' or 'authentic' are related words increasingly to be found attached to terms like 'assessment activity' or 'classroom task'. But there is an interesting and productive tension here: teaching is an avowedly artificial activity, the providing (as I see it) of opportunities both to encounter and experience moments that are not easily or sometimes never available in the self-styled 'real' world (see Pimm, 1995).

This quality – deliberate artificiality – of the teaching need not be transmitted to the hoped-for associated learning. Artificial need not mean fake or false. The key element for me is that the tasks described in the book offer the possibility of productive intellectual and emotional engagement. And the projects reported here provide ample evidence of that: not because they are 'real-world', but because they are real.

Nel Noddings (1994), in a critical commentary on the American NCTM document *Everybody counts*, observes:

> But a particular problem that is 'real-world' in the sense that adult human beings grapple with it may not be 'real' at all in the school setting.... A problem is real for actual people when they want or need to solve it.
>
> (p. 97)

There are further resonances here. Rena asks (p. 3) 'What is it that makes what we do or create "real"?', and then proceeds to offer a number of characteristics of real things. Bill too, on page 12, talks of his feelings of not seeing himself as a 'real' mathematician, while providing contrary evidence and discussion for us. And Eileen, on p. 10, tells of a parental enquiry: "When [are you] going to start real maths?" And Rena again, in both Chapter 1 and Chapter 6, talks about the human antonym of feeling real, namely feeling like an impostor.

Another antonym of 'real' is 'toy', something associated with children 'just playing'. Valerie Walkerdine (1981) has commented insightfully on primary school children's sense of rupture between 'work' and 'play' in mathematics. And Janet Ainley (1988a) has produced a telling critique of the notion that 'games are necessarily good' in mathematics, in a book chapter entitled 'Playing games and real mathematics'. One further tension that arises between Rena and Bill in Chapter 4 is their involvement and engagement (or otherwise) with 'games and puzzles'.

There is an often-heard teacher comment: "I want/need to make maths fun for my pupils". A sense of 'fun', it seems to me, is a side-product of creative engagement, not the main event. Things can be 'fun' without being worth attending to. Fun can also be irrelevant to things well worth attending to in a serious but not necessarily solemn manner. As one of the children in Eileen's classroom gleefully observed in reaction to a challenge: 'It's hard fun'. One characteristic of the real is that it is worthy of our attention.

There is much that has been written and will be written again about 'integration' of mathematics in schools. But to frame this book in terms of 'the issue of curricular integration' seems:

(a) to acknowledge there is a problem ('dis-integration' perhaps?) that needs addressing;
(b) to suggest that there must be a particular problem with mathematics.

A specific and strong focus on 'integration' in mathematics education certainly strongly suggests that mathematics' separateness is the norm (and therefore need not be explained?). It does not explore how the current situation and perceptions came to be. Nevertheless, there is much for writers on curriculum integration of mathematics in this book.

Too often talk of integration falls into the integrating of X into Y (art into maths or language work into social studies, for example). Thematic or topic work is sometimes presumed to take care of mathematics along with every other subject area. But this can easily degenerate into the two poles of Ainley's (1988b) 'Dead birds' (throw over the whole lesson to work on the dead bird a child found on the way to school) and 'Easter bunnies' (the arithmetic problems are the same as before, but are written on bunny outlines as part of an Easter theme).

David Jardine (1995) writes:

> Blaming teachers for engaging their children in such trite activities in the name of curriculum integration belies the fact that we are all 'witnessing the inevitable outcome of a logic [of fragmentation, severance and dis-integration] that is already centuries old and that is being played out in our lifetime' (Berman, 1983, p. 23). ... Such classroom activities should therefore not be taken up as occasions for blame, but as interpretative opportunities that give us all ways to address how we might make our pedagogical conduct more well integrated and whole.
>
> (p. 263)

The word 'integration' is very close to a number of others with resonant connections: 'integral', 'integrity' and 'integer', all offering images of wholeness and, perhaps, seamlessness. This book offers many instances of high-level wholeness: in attitude, perseverance, problem solving, internal and external challenge and reflection. These are some of the central, deeply educational commonalities across projects that could form the basis for part of a powerful mathematics curriculum. The integration that is most in evidence is in the work and the learning, over time.

Then there is the seldom acknowledged difficulty of knowing when mathematics is actually being done, and whether it matters that work one person sees as mathematical, another classifies as something else (art, music, science, even simply 'thinking'). There is a real danger of discipline imperialism here, with mathematics the most potentially imperialist of all. It is not just in teaching contexts that problems over these boundaries, demarcations and distinctions come into play.

My strong belief – and one that I recognise as inherent in this work – is that mathematics is a particular discipline, with its own ways of seeing, stressing and ignoring: ways that need to be acquired if the great potential inherent in offering mathematics in schools is to be realised. But there is still an underexplored question, that of 'Why is mathematics worth teaching, why is mathematics worth offering to pupils?' This book provides a substantial contribution to this question.

Too often in response to such accounts of particular classroom investigations and explorations, the question asked is: 'What is generalisable?' This is a mathematical question in some ways. As with Rena's attempt to characterise part of 'the real', I think endeavouring to delineate some features of 'such projects as these' might prove to be a worthwhile future venture. However, far better, I feel, is the question: 'What can others hope to take away with them from this book to use for their own ends?' In other words, what is appropriable? What resonates for the reader?

Resonance is an issue that can be answered by a challenging question of quite a different sort: 'Who is this book for?' (and many implausible answers to this question are frequently offered in prefaces). I want to propose that relatively novice teachers will find descriptions of class activities and insights into particular ways of working with pupils on mathematics through projects, the like of which are very hard to find in print. Experienced teachers may find sufficient challenge or innovation to their established patterns of classroom operation to invigorate an exploration of their own teaching repertoire.

Mathematics educators will gain access to an articulate report by sophisticated and aware observers of their own and other classrooms, as well as of each other and themselves – by means of words from authors who are prepared to reveal and contemplate the difficulties as well as the rewards of lived mathematical experience. All of these potential readers (and more – parents? arts educators? teacher educators?) can read of the experiences of this class of children working and thinking mathematically while creating things.

The final striking feature for me is one of time. I was surprised to find that, despite the wealth and quality of work reported on here, Rena spent relatively little time in Eileen's classroom over the year. The projects reported arose from an hour's work every Thursday afternoon (in a period when in previous years Eileen would offer a choice of mathematical activities), together with some lunch times when pupils got particularly engaged in something, as well as occasional half and whole days.

This observation may release or increase tension in a teacher-reader. For there is some exceptional thinking and doing by young children reported in these pages. And, at times, we all react to exceptions by excluding rather than accepting them ('monster-barring' is Lakatos' (1976) resonant term for this process within mathematics; 'excluding outliers' describes a similar activity in statistics). This can result in not having to think about the unexpected, and therefore not encounter its power to disturb.

A feeling of release can arise from a sense of 'I could try this too', as Eileen herself comments in places. This is not an enterprise that requires a complete upheaval in classroom setting or even operation. It is containable. But beware. The excitement of mathematical thinking is contagious: 'hard fun' can prove addictive.

To some extent, Bill, in his role of intimate outsider, has provided us with an instance of what he found in the accounts of the other two writers. But his connections are necessarily particular, as ours will also be. I think authors always need to address the question: 'Why might readers be interested in this book?'; but it also is up to us, as readers, to be attuned to what the book has to offer us. Because, as the children's work bears out time and again, it is frequently the unexpected, the unanticipated, which can result in the most productive avenues, giving rise to that most elusive educational grail, a genuine encounter with the real.

David Pimm
Vancouver
August 1996

Acknowledgements

Readers of this book will soon realise that this is the only page on which we, the three authors, write in a single 'unified' voice.

Indeed, perhaps this is the only place where our views are one: the people we thank here are friends and colleagues to us all.

One always owes a debt of thanks to one's partners, and in this case, the debt to Gary William Rasberry, David Pimm, and Annie Barwise goes beyond support of a personal nature. It is true that without their encouragement the book would not have been completed, but in addition, Gary and David acted as editors of our work, constantly reading, suggesting, modifying, extending, interrogating and affirming our words.

We feel deep gratitude to the pupils who so willingly participated with us during the 1992–3 year in room 108. Our thanks also goes to their parents, for suspending disbelief (for at least one afternoon a week) in their own expectations of school mathematics, for encouraging us to continue as the year progressed, and for generally endorsing the work we undertook. We are thankful too for the support of Graham Nixon, principal of the school at the time that this work took place.

We would like to express our appreciation to our colleagues at the University of British Columbia and Queen's University. Our thanks goes to Corina Koch and Jillian DeJean for their assistance in compiling photographs and samples of the children's work. In addition, in the latter stages of writing, this work was supported in part by funds from the Natural Sciences and Engineering Research Council of Canada, and the Faculty of Education at Queen's University.

In an undertaking of this sort, family members contribute in ways that are significant, and often unknown to them at the time. We thank Kate Higginson, Robin Phillips, and Jaclyn Phillips for their patience and love.

We also acknowledge the importance of our own evolving relationships with one another. To say that this book was a mutual undertaking perhaps belies the depth of growth that we all experienced as we saw this book to completion. Rena will forever remain grateful to Eileen for her willingness to travel in directions that were new and challenging and to Bill for his readiness to discuss ideas mathematical. Eileen recalls the magic and inspiration of interacting with Rena, both in and outside the classroom, and the specialness of meeting Bill for the first time, feeling as though she already knew him. Bill thanks Eileen for the rich glimpses into the lives of children, and Rena for her persistence in pushing him forward as the writing took hold.

Finally, we are grateful to the staff at Routledge, and to the reviewers who responded so positively and helpfully and insightfully to this somewhat unusual work.

Rena Upitis
Eileen Phillips
Bill Higginson

August 1996

Chapter 1

Introduction

'Oh good, it's time for maths!'

RENA UPITIS: researcher

I was one of the lucky ones. Unlike most of my high school friends, I looked forward to mathematics classes. For me, mathematics was simple – useless, but simple. I sailed through high school algebra, trigonometry and geometry, rarely receiving less than 100 per cent on my assignments and exams. But maths remained at best a comparatively harmless way to spend a few hours in school – it was not boring, but it did not exactly fill my life with excitement. My passion was – and is – music. The only time mathematics held any fascination for me was when I saw some connections between music and mathematics, and these were connections I made only rarely.

When I entered university, I began to accumulate a hodge-podge of courses towards a liberal arts degree, majoring in psychology and dabbling in philosophy along the way. Music did not find its way into my university studies – in fact, for a couple of years, I abandoned it almost completely. But, oddly enough, I was only one course short of a minor in mathematics. Somehow I managed to accumulate enough credits in linear algebra, statistics, and engineering calculus to hang out in the basement of the maths building, punching long series of weird symbols into the computer, without raising anyone's suspicions that I might be an impostor. But even though I was 'doing maths', and at the university level no less, I did not feel like a mathematician, at least, not in the way that I felt like a musician.

By the time I started a graduate degree in education, I had embraced music wholeheartedly, carrying out thesis research on how children might become composers using computer tools (well, maybe maths did not disappear completely). That was well over a decade ago. At that time, Bill Higginson, one of my mathematics professors (and a co-author of this book), suggested I take on some explorations in mathematics, linking my love of music with the beauty he saw in mathematics. I did not do so at the time (do students ever really listen to the advice of their professors?), but Bill and I nevertheless had many discussions over the years about the nature of mathematics.

Our discussions have deeply influenced my thinking about maths, and about music as well. How could I help but be affected by a man who sees the mathematics in a milk carton, in the tiles running down the hallway, in the trim on an antique wooden cabinet, and in a snowflake? And how could I not notice his strange and wonderful collection of maths books? The books he collects just do not look like the textbooks we used in high school and in university. Instead of the recognisable (and dull) titles like *Linear Algebra I* and *Linear Algebra II*, they have inviting titles like *Islands of Truth: a Mathematical Mystery Cruise* (Peterson, 1990), *Number Words and Number Symbols: A Cultural History of Numbers* (Menninger, 1969), and *Connections: the Geometric Bridge Between Art and Science* (Kappraff, 1991). It is not as if these books do not talk about algebra and geometry – they do. It is that these books do not use the learning of algebra and geometry as the endpoints in mathematics, but rather, as tools for creation – tools that are needed to make beautiful tessellating patterns or to understand the allure of a snowflake.

In our conversations, Bill often mentioned that symmetry is one of the 'big ideas' in mathematics – well, it is a big idea in music as well. So how are the two related? And what about transformations? Can a piece of music played backwards be related to a reflection of a geometric figure? Is repetition as important in creating pattern in mathematics as it is in the visual arts? These are questions I carried with me as we began to formulate the projects described in this book.

I also carried with me considerable experience working with children from my years as a music teacher, both in private music lessons and in troubled but thriving inner-city schools in Canada and the United States. Having taught children from privileged settings in the private music context as well as working with children who lived in transient situations and in cultures different from my own, I had grown to realise that there were common themes in learning environments that, at first blush, seem very different.

If I was able to respond to children's views, create environments where they could find forms of personal expression, and stimulate situations where rich and deep thinking could occur, then, in my experience, it was just as likely that a ten-year-old who was living from hand to mouth would be able to compose a satisfying piece of music as the ten-year-old whose father drove her to weekly piano lessons in the family's BMW. As a result of these prior experiences, I had some strongly supported notions of how children learn and make meaning, particularly when some of the traditional trappings of classroom life are abandoned.

In my work with children as musicians and composers (Upitis, 1990a, 1992), it became clear to me that children become most deeply invested in their own creations and learning when they feel that they are making something *real*. Like the hero of *The Velveteen Rabbit* (Williams, 1989), they want to know what is real, how to be real, how to make something real.

Children know from an early age that there is 'kids' stuff' and 'real stuff', and they want to be a part of the latter much more than of the former. Before looking at what makes something real in mathematics, I take the liberty of eavesdropping on the conversation between the Velveteen Rabbit and the Skin Horse, a toy that knows the meaning of real.

'What is REAL?', asked the Rabbit one day, when they were lying side by side by the nursery fender, before Nana came to tidy the room. 'Does it mean having things that buzz inside you and a stick-out handle?'

'Real isn't how you are made', said the Skin Horse. 'It's a thing that happens to you.' ...

'Does it hurt?', asked the Rabbit.

'Sometimes', said the Skin Horse, for he was always truthful. 'When you are Real you don't mind being hurt.'

'Does it happen all at once, like being wound-up', he asked, 'or bit by bit?'

'It doesn't happen all at once', said the Skin Horse. 'You become. It takes a long time.... Generally, by the time you are Real, most of your hair has been loved off, and your eyes drop out, and you get loose in the joints and very shabby. But these things don't matter at all, because once you are Real you can't be ugly, except to people who don't understand ... once you are Real you can't become unreal again. It lasts for always.'

The Rabbit sighed. He thought it would be a long time before this magic called Real happened to him. He longed to become Real, to know what it felt like; and yet, the idea of growing shabby and losing his eyes and whiskers was rather sad. He wished that he could become it without these uncomfortable things happening to him.

What is it that makes what we do or create 'real'? I think there are several features of creations that children – and adults – consider real. They need not be present in every case, but often real things have at least two or three of the features I am about to describe.

Real things are often beautiful; they have an aesthetic appeal. The beauty frequently lies in the materials used – creating a watercolour on top quality rag paper with a grainy texture is more appealing, more real, than the same painting crafted on a piece of white newsprint (like the paper often used by children in Kindergarten classes). Similarly, children gravitate towards manipulable maths materials that have some appeal, either in colour or feel.

In the first project described in this book, I used a number of different kinds of ceramic tiles to explore tessellations. I also had some brightly-coloured construction paper shapes and pattern blocks that the children could use to create their own tessellating patterns. Invariably, they chose the more aesthetically appealing materials – large and smooth ceramic tiles were chosen over small plastic tiles; pattern block triangles were chosen over the same shapes cut from construction paper.

Beautiful things that are real are so regardless of who has made them. One of my music pupils, at the age of ten, composed a trio for clarinet, flute, and piano. The composition was remarkable, not because it was composed by a ten-year-old, but because it was delicately crafted – it was Real. A couple of people, on hearing this composition, exclaimed: 'That is amazing for a ten-year-old'. Their amazement came not from the fact that a ten-year-old composed a piece of music, but rather, from the feeling that the music was worth performing for its own sake, regardless of the age of the composer.

Sometimes children will add something to an artifact to make it look more real. In an engineering structures problem, where pupils were challenged to create a bridge from spaghetti, one pupil added graffiti to the bridge, in order to make it more than just a science exercise. He commented: 'Real bridges have graffiti'. But the bridge was already real in another way – it was able to support a considerable weight. This brings me to another feature of real things; they can be very large or capable of holding something heavy, or conversely, very tiny – like a computer chip. I doubt that the pupil would have added the graffiti to his bridge if the bridge could not sustain a large weight. Because it held a considerable load, it was real already – he was merely drawing attention to its 'realness'.

Real things can also be functional. The paper jewellery creations described later in this book are both functional and aesthetically pleasing, and these features together make them real. Something that is unique – a discovery – can also be real, even in its rough form. There is a fine example of this in the tessellations project, where a child was so excited about a tessellating pattern that he produced that he claimed it as his own. He wrote: 'I discoverded it' across the top of the page where he had sketched the pattern.

Real things, as the Velveteen Rabbit found, often take an effort to produce – a physical, mental, and emotional effort (or as one child put it, 'It's hard fun'). It therefore takes a good deal of time to produce real things, to make real discoveries. And of course, real things are often produced when working with others. Some of the most beautiful music I have heard children compose has been the result of a collaborative effort amongst the children and an adult composer – an apprenticeship model of learning. This learning through doing and apprenticing is eloquently described by the Inuit scholar, Louis-Jacques Dorais, who translated the words of Taamusi Qumaq talking about the schools that white people from the 'south' have instituted in Canada's north in the following way.

A house is a school, it is run by Qallunaat [white people]. This one has people who are taught, many of them, who learn only through words. Also one person can be a school too, when one who is really working, who is trying to do something real, is looking at this person when (s)he is working.

(Cited in Stairs, 1994, p. 67)

The work that we describe in the chapters that follow was real both to us and to the children. Much of what the children produced was truly beautiful – silk cards with tessellating patterns, music compositions, paper jewels. It took many hours for them to create their works. Because the children were engaged in real explorations and creations, a great deal of learning took place as well.

When Bill Higginson and I first talked about an exploratory venture that would involve a classroom teacher and pupils over an extended period of time – a full school year – he and I agreed that it was crucial to work with someone who would find such an undertaking enriching rather than a hindrance. Late one August afternoon, sitting in Bill's office talking about my upcoming sabbatical leave, he and I realised that the time had come to embark on this long-talked-about enterprise, as I prepared to leave Ontario to spend my sabbatical year in Vancouver, British Columbia.

We began to focus our discussion on what qualities I might look for in a teacher, and on how I might find such a person. I was planning to spend many hours in the classroom, and it was important to me that I become a 'regular' instead of a 'visitor'. But I knew that in order to become a member of the classroom community, I had to work with a teacher who would in some ways see me as a teaching partner (although at that time I was thinking in terms of working separately with a group of children), and who would regard our time together as something worthwhile not only for the children, but for herself as well. This meant finding a teacher who would regard the 'research' project as an integral part of the classroom experience, rather than an extra thing to add to an already busy schedule.

Bill and I are keenly aware, from our own experiences and from years of observation, that teachers work extremely hard. Many primary teachers rightly complain about having to teach too many subjects, noting that as the years go by, more subjects and issues are added to an already full curriculum plate. Although I believe that we have to include such issues as environmental science, gender, violence, and anti-racist education in the curriculum, this inclusion need not, and indeed, *should* not be in ways that make each subject separate and distinct.

I want to be able to teach mathematics because I understand music and language; I also want the activities we choose to be culturally broad and environmentally respectful. Teachers who see subjects as connected will find that the work we describe is not extra teaching, but rather, deeper teaching of what they already do well.

When I described this research project to a colleague at the University of British Columbia, she suggested I speak with Eileen Phillips, a teacher in one of the local Vancouver schools, and so it began.[1] We met after school one day, over a cup of tea in a nearly deserted staffroom. I was delighted to find that Eileen was just the teacher I was hoping to find.

Eileen is passionately interested in the teaching and learning of mathematics. She enjoys the challenge of trying to present mathematical concepts in ways that are meaningful to the children, and at the same time, works at gaining a rich sense of their individual ways of learning about mathematics. Her teaching of mathematics already made extensive use of manipulative materials; in fact, I have never seen maths textbooks used in her classroom. Rather, she asks that children record their findings, describe strategies they develop for solving problems, and keep a journal on their mathematical interests and work. But more on this later, when Eileen tells you about her classroom herself.

This is perhaps a good moment to speak more about the structure of this book. As David Pimm indicated in his preface, it is unusual to present a trio of voices; in this case, mine, Bill's, and Eileen's. Both Bill and I have considerable experience conducting research in classroom settings. But one of the failings of some of our earlier work is that the classroom teacher's voice has been missing. While we have both been careful to represent classroom teachers' views, it has always been in the form of 'researcher as ventriloquist'.[2] That is, while we have carefully recorded and quoted teachers' words, the teachers have not written as contributing authors. With teachers' voices only as background, important parts of the whole have been missing. Here our trio, although at times uneven and unrehearsed, will piece together a composition that we hope is rich in the telling.

Of course, there are background voices as well – the children's chorus. While we have not devoted full chapter sections to children's writing, there are journal excerpts and quotations, drawings and photographs, scattered throughout that add harmony to our score. The children in this project were twenty-seven youngsters, aged from 7 to 10 years, in a Grade 3 and 4 combined class. While I spent most of my time working with the Grade 3 children, all of the children were involved in the projects that Eileen and I concocted. The Grade 3 pupils I worked with comprised a mixed group in terms of gender, academic ability, maturity, and ethnicity.

The exploratory research work was described to the children and to their parents as 'maths projects'. Our plan was to engage the children in projects that combined mathematics with visual arts and/or music, so that children would have opportunities to create artistic works through the manipulation of mathematical ideas. We called our work 'projects', to suggest that the products would take time to develop and complete – these were not one-period, one-class activities. We explained that there would be only four or five such projects undertaken over the school year.

The children were eager participants – I do not now doubt that their general liking of and receptiveness to mathematics was due in large part to Eileen's 'regular' maths programme, which had been running for a couple of weeks when I first arrived, with Eileen exploring their knowledge through mathematical games and problems. So, the notion of doing 'maths with Miss Upitis on Thursday afternoons' was not received with trepidation, but with eagerness.

There is one final issue I would like to raise by way of my personal introduction to this book. Many people have an aversion to mathematics, and there is a plethora of research specifically indicating that many girls and women find mathematics dull, irrelevant, difficult, and even repulsive; and further, that they are socialised to feel this way.[3] In the early 1990s, when we were just embarking on this researching-teaching venture, I was appalled to hear that the *Teen-Talk Barbie* doll, in keeping with her many questionable qualities, was now putting her permanently arched foot in her mouth by saying that: 'Math[s] class is tough'. As the Mattel doll manufacturers were quick to point out, this was only one of 270 possible messages; all of the others were positive, portraying women in a more favourable light. This makes the 'Math[s] class is tough' message even more troublesome – it was not one of many potentially damaging comments – it was the *only* one.

Teachers of mathematics are constantly fighting stereotyping of this sort. And things are beginning to change. Coincident with the Barbie message in the early 1990s was a growth in projects and approaches that began to address both the stereotype and its effects. These included projects at the teacher education level (for example, Kleinfeld and Yerian, 1991), increased emphasis on 'family mathematics' curriculum approaches where ways of making maths in the home setting that include girls and their mothers, as well as male family members, are explored (Stenmark *et al.*, 1986), and research and development projects aimed at developing electronic tools to support girls' understanding and interest in mathematics.

An example of the latter is the Electronic Games for Education in Maths and Science (E-GEMS) project, based at the University of British Columbia (Klawe, 1994; Koch and Upitis, 1996). While we have yet to see the widespread effects of projects and approaches such as these, it is encouraging that many people have not only acknowledged that a problem exists, but are beginning to understand new ways of promoting interest in mathematics through authentic activities that include learning through social interaction.

As a concluding observation, I would suggest that one of the most important ways of confronting the stereotype that girls find mathematics difficult or inaccessible is to recognise and name the mathematical work that girls and women are doing as mathematical work (Upitis, 1995a). Bill, Eileen, and I have seen many instances where children are doing work that we recognise as mathematics, but which they, and/or their teachers, do not. Invariably, this work is called something else like 'project time' or 'special art' or simply 'games', but in fact, has just as much or more of a claim to be labelled as mathematics as does the work that is readily called this by the children. Nothing could have made me happier than hearing Jennifer, one of the children, exclaim on my second day: 'Oh good! It's time for math[s]'. Even one afternoon of messing around with tiles and tessellations was enough for her to recognise the mathematics in our play, and to label it as such. But the story of the tessellations project itself remains for the next chapter.

EILEEN PHILLIPS: teacher

I, too, was one of the lucky ones. Elementary school was, for the most part, filled with 'easy arithmetic'; secondary school, with rules to be followed that would let one in on the mystery of algebra and geometry, if one's memory was focused enough. I disliked the presentation of the content and yet, somehow, I was lucky enough to maintain a love for, and an interest in, the subject of mathematics itself.

Early in my teaching career – over twenty years ago – I was fortunate to be involved in a mathematics interest group headed by John Trivett and Sandy Dawson of Simon Fraser University. We were a small group of practising teachers, university lecturers, and student teachers who met regularly to discuss what we were teaching in maths, and why and how we were teaching it. We spent hours playing with Cuisenaire rods, solving mathematical games and puzzles, looking for patterns in numbers, and discussing the ideas of educators like Caleb Gattegno (1970) and Edward de Bono (1971). We called ourselves the *Learning By Heart* group, and we took our name and all its implications very seriously.

Our lives changed, complications arose, the curriculum took on a new 'back to basics' focus, and we gradually disbanded. My teaching style changed. I moved away from manipulatives, away from maths stations, and away from maths projects. I moved towards individual instruction, allowing pupils to work their way through the textbook. Still, I seemed to spend a good deal of time monitoring progress, and assessing independent under- standing of the text. But how I missed the liveliness of manipulative play and the heated discussions of maths the 'old' way.

When I reinstated a maths games period into my classroom, I felt better immediately. Next, after teaching to the whole class, I began encouraging pupils to break into groups for working out and presenting solutions to problems posed. However, I still felt obliged to 'do the text'. I would assign pages and give weekly tests to monitor progress. Nevertheless, the pupils seemed to enjoy maths. They did well on standardised tests, the parents were happy that their children had homework, and my colleagues told me that they were pleased with how my pupils retained mathematical concepts over the long summer break.

However, I felt that I was holding back. I was focusing too much on being accountable to people outside the classroom. I wanted to focus on the pupils and on what they might need to know. Even when I moved to a combination of textbook work with manipulative materials and methods from my early days, I remained unsatisfied.

I started the school year (in which the work we describe in this book took place) determined to continue to teach in a more learner-focused way, and to continue to develop my teaching strategies further. I had already decided I would value my own expertise and knowledge and use a variety of teaching tools and assessment methods. The *Mathematics, a Way of Thinking* course I had taken over the summer inspired me. Also, I had started to interact with another like-minded teacher on the staff. Once again, I had a support system and a vision of mathematics beyond the textbook.

Timing is very powerful. I had recently started a masters course in mathematics teaching at the University of British Columbia, and I was feeling wonderful. At UBC, I was being exposed to ideas and discussions that not only mirrored my thinking and methods, but extended them.

My professor, Ann Anderson, asked if I would be willing to have a researcher whose interest was in the links amongst maths, music, and art. I found many maths/music/art connections flooding into my awareness and felt immediately intrigued. At the time, Ann indicated Rena wanted to have a smallish group on a pull-out basis. Between the time of the initial suggestion and my first meeting with Rena, I found myself wondering what I was in for. I often have other adults in my classroom – student teachers, parents, and colleagues – but somehow this seemed different. How much time would she want? How much was I going to expose myself? How much control would I have? Would my pupils really be gaining a worthwhile experience from this? And why did I want to add another thing to my already complicated life? 'Relax, you can always say no', I assured myself.

Then I met Rena. It is hard to describe the energy that flows from Rena. It is not loud and pulsating, not showy or pushy, yet it has a presence. It was this presence that grabbed my imagination and curiosity immediately. I really wanted to work with this woman. I felt no hesitation. We planned our timetable, the presentation to the parents, and discussed the feasibility of what she wanted to do. I could not locate an area in the school for her to work in, and so decided on initial strategies of how we could work within the same classroom, at the same time, each doing what we wanted without disrupting each other. But soon after that first meeting we got caught up in each other's hopes and plans, and began weaving our projects and activities in a complementary fashion.

My class, in September, was composed of eleven Grade 3 and sixteen Grade 4 pupils. There were ten girls (six in Grade 3, and only four in Grade 4), and seventeen boys (five in Grade 3, and twelve in Grade 4). Their ages ranged from seven to ten years over the course of the school year, and their ability range spanned several grades. All were from middle-class back-grounds and were well-cared-for in their home settings. As with other classes I have taught, I found that some pupils were extremely independent, some had been pampered, some were opinionated, some were motivated, some were 'into school', some enjoyed showing off, some were quiet – and the list goes on. Oh yes – on an interest graph that we did early in September, no one chose mathematics as their favourite subject.

These choices were not unusual. On 'start-of-the-year' graphs, pupils often identify art, physical education, and, occasionally, reading as their favourite school subjects, regardless of the background of the pupils. Like Rena, I have taught children from widely varied socio-economic circumstances. For most of my teaching career, prior to teaching in the predominantly affluent catchment area we describe in this book, I have worked with classes of pupils for a majority of whom English is their second language. In these schools, many of the parents struggle to support their families' economic needs and educational aspirations.

Also, class sizes have ranged from eighteen (in one lucky year!) to close to forty pupils in a room. In my career as a schoolteacher, class sizes have correlated more closely with political expenditures and priorities than with the socio-ecomonic status of the parents. Nevertheless, the class we describe was an undoubtedly privileged one. For a range of reasons, this class stands out as unique in my memory.

The class was set up so we could purposely think of ourselves as room 108, rather than Grade 3s and Grade 4s separately. I chose to teach whole-class, open-ended lessons in all subjects, and often used small working groups for co-operative projects. Each working group had a mixture of both boys and girls from both grades. One exception to this proved to be social studies, later in the year, and another was the maths projects. Rena would teach the Grade 3 pupils and I would teach the rest during maths projects sessions. At times, we would blend the groups and lead them together.

Before I close this introduction, I feel compelled to talk about my use/non-use of the textbook during the year that Rena spent in my classroom. I know that Rena felt I never used one, but the truth is that I did (and do) from time to time. As is my custom, I began the year with this class collecting data and recording findings on graphs. A lot of time was spent discussing how this was maths, why this was maths, and what we were learning. Initially, the pupils felt this work was fun, but they needed help understanding what was mathematical about it. Early in the year, I also started the class writing about their maths lessons, games, and activities in informal journal entries. I wanted to create an orientation to mathematics that would extend beyond book maths and worksheets.

However, around the end of October, I started to get some not-so-subtle enquiries from parents about my maths curriculum. 'When', one parent wanted to know, was I 'going to start real maths? What is my child doing playing with beans in cups?' Another asked why we were not as far along as another class was in the textbook. Rather than fight head on, I accommodated. I decided that the pupils could pursue textbook explorations as a sort of combination maths review and introduction to long-term self-pacing. I created a list of pages, instructed the pupils to do five questions per page, showed them how to mark their work, built in some accountability, and gave them a timeline. All but four completed the assignment successfully. Occasionally, I also used problem-solving booklets and enrichment worksheets. I tend to be rather eclectic. If I see something I think I can work with, I use it.

As I sat at my computer writing this opening section, I found myself wondering if my readiness to embark on this project came through. It is my hope that classroom teachers reading this account will feel encouraged to respond to or even seek an opportunity like this one, regardless of their teaching circumstances and even if they were to experience some apprehension, as I did. This experience would have been valuable to me if I had been teaching quite a different sort of class at the time or if I had found my own collaborator. Classroom teachers are continually developing more effective ways to teach children. One of the surest ways of doing this is to become a teacher-researcher in collaboration with others.

Each year, there are incidents that stand out and become transformed into part of my practice. Some of my most significant learning comes from reflection on specific incidents (both in my practice and in the practice of others), not from general accounts about classrooms or educational research. When talking about this to Rena, she remarked that, as a researcher, she cares less about generalisability than making connections. Thus, in this book, we emphasise the uniqueness and specifics of the learning experiences we shared because we believe that it is through attention to the specific that practices are affirmed and/or altered.

BILL HIGGINSON: mathematician

Enter the third and final character in our narrative. First, there was Rena the researcher, then Eileen the teacher, and now, myself, Bill the mathematician. Starkly isolated, 'mathematician' seems a blunt and potentially pretentious identification and my first impulse is to demur, 'Well, not really'. But if we acknowledge that no single descriptor can ever snugly fit the richnesses of our multifold selves, let me accept the claim and contribute to the following pages as best I can from a mathematical perspective.

This voice is, as you will have already noted, a different one. It differs in time, space, gender and experience from the ones that have come before. Rena and Eileen have forged their words interactively from that furnace of ideas, actions, intentions, and insights that is Eileen's classroom. My contact has been distanced, symbolic – mediated by several of the potent devices of modern communication technology. The story emerged over the course of ten months – by modem, by videotape, by face-to-face conversations, by computer disc, by fax, by paper, and by telephone. A story of excitement, of imagination, of growth. And now the three of us are engaged in reflecting on what happened and why, to probe for meanings and significance, and to speculate about implications, imperatives and possibilities.

This task seems to me, somewhat paradoxically perhaps, to be simultaneously natural and quite difficult. Natural, and exciting, because it deals with children making, learning, and knowing. And that, at least with respect to mathematics, is supposed to be my stock in trade. As a mathematics educator

– among other things, a teacher of teachers – I occupy that somewhat lonely and hazardous ground between mathematics teacher and research mathematician. Half-caste, hybrid, neither finned nor feathered, easily and frequently incurring the ire and indignation of both sides of the family tree.

Perhaps that is where the difficulty arises. Removed from day-to-day contact with challenging adolescents, I am considered by mathematics teachers as out of touch with the realities of the classroom. By not appearing in the pages of prestigious research mathematics journals, I am considered not a 'real' mathematician by those whose work appears there. Yet, in theory, my work both informs and is informed by the activities of these two seldom-overlapping groups.

Even as a mathematics educator and researcher, the kind of enquiry described here may well be regarded with scepticism by some, built as it is on stories of personal experience. What might probing and inferring be without questionnaires, validity, and elegant statistics? What of objectivity? Is one's scientific lab coat to evaporate as in an inferior French farce, leaving one to face the hostile world clad only in heart-festooned boxer briefs? Be brave mid-career man! They say there is a new world out there built on honesty, trust and openness. It is perhaps worth a try.

I cannot remember exactly when mathematics became more than mere mechanics for me. As a preschooler, chubby, precocious, and co-ordinationally challenged, books were my great love. I read early and often, beginning habits that have endured for decades. Nature and nurture joined forces to ensure an appreciation for the world of words. Mother, straight from a Rockwell painting, truncated a promising beginning in nursing to follow that career-of-the-era – homemaker. Midst the cooking, cleaning and caring there was much time for rocking and reading.

My father, first a teacher in a small northern railroad town, and later, a pre-war school principal, was a poet of no mean talent. Master of metaphor, vocabulary wizard, his summer-school pleasure as he toiled toward his bachelor's degree during the years of the depression, was to read the Oxford English Dictionary, volume by long volume. 'Not much of a plot', he would say later with a shy, nerd-before-his-time, smile. And later, when I myself discovered that mathematically-special word 'set', I wondered if he had read every one of the twenty-three pages required to squeeze the meanings from that deceptively simple triad of letters.

From my pre-school socialisation only one mathematical incident lingers, but it is, for me, significant. In the small town where we lived I had made friends with a boy called Andy Warner. Even among the rubes of rural Ontario there was a social pecking order, and I was dimly aware of my mother's unvoiced concerns about my fraternisation with 'one of the Warners'. Innocent as I was, and with society yet to generate its wealth of terms to describe the various poverties of the Warners' class, I found Andy a robust and lively companion.

As luck would have it, Andy was a few months older than me, and one leafy day in early September he joined most of the other children and my father in heading off for school. Thus, doubly abandoned, I was left to tricycle disconsolately about my one square block turf. It was one of my first lessons in the injustice of bureaucracies for I felt that Andy had almost none of the fascination with symbols that I had.

After the first day (for he was one of the 'What? You mean I have to go again!' children), he would, I am sure, willingly have traded places. It was not to be, however, and I was left to my square tricycling and to curse the fates that had made me a November baby. From this metaphysical funk it was but a short step to the depths of infinity by way of the apparently reasonable question: 'What is the biggest number in the world?'

This was the teaser I hit Andy with one autumnal afternoon as he trudged from school to home. It was to his credit that he gave this philosophical toughie considerable thought. And when, with eyes rolling skyward, he finally gave his clenched-fist, 'best-shot' response (I no longer recall exactly what he said – it was of the order of 'Ninety-nine million and mutter, mutter' – the critical insight that had come during my solitary musings was that it really did not matter at all what was initially proposed), I realised that I had probably underestimated the mathematical abilities of my scruffy mate. It was not, however, a moment for character speculation.

Toreador-quick I topped his game effort with a triumphant, 'Plus one!' Resistance was brief – sounds started, but before they became speech the tension left his body, and probably not for the last time Andy realised that in some situations no matter how hard you try it just is not going to be good enough.

Memories of school mathematics have none of that vividness. I was told frequently, both directly and indirectly, that I was very good at it, and by the criteria of the time I suppose I was. The rules were simple and potent: please those in power, and outperform your peers. There was, as I recall, no particular malice on my part in my classroom quickness. This was my terrain. The patient looks I gave my classmates, as they slogged through what were to me the simplest of sums and differences, paralleled exactly the glances I received from them as I fumbled and panted my way through various playground challenges.

To the teacher I was the classic 'pet' – diligent, dependable, eager-to-please. From my perspective the 'us' and 'them' classroom alliances, at least for things scholastic, clearly bracketed me with the teacher. Was it not the case that my test was always marked first just to make sure that she had not made any mistakes?

After the large tadpole in a tiny puddle days of high school, the crowded, competitive, university pond was an abrupt and sobering surprise. The 'Honours Maths' degree programme had in its favour a modest, if geekishly-tinged, social cachet, and the great merit of demanding neither afternoon-devouring labs nor nightmarish, end-of-semester term papers. Unfortunately, it also had arid, mind-numbing courses, based on texts saturated with incomprehensible symbols and fiendish exercises, and instructors who all too frequently could have been the model for the archetypal mathematics professor who 'says A, writes B, and means C, when it should be D' (Polya, 1971, p. 22).

Intuitively adopting a rawly Darwinian strategy – stay in the shadows, do not take risks, do not panic – I emerged, four years after entry, bruised but not completely bowed. That teaching should beckon as a vocation was probably not a surprise. The demand was high, it was a calling I knew well from my family background, and the prospect of working closely with young people was one that appealed to me.

It was shortly after graduation, during a two-year stint in the highlands of East Africa as a 'Peace Corpse' teacher (as my students phrased it), that the mysteries of the university mathematics curriculum began to succumb to large chunks of reading time and my bookish strengths. To my mixed delight (I can understand this stuff) and dismay (why did I not find this out sooner?), I found that the dazzlingly dense concepts of my undergraduate work in courses like linear algebra and vector calculus needed only gifted expositor-teachers like Warwick Sawyer (1957, 1963) or Richard Courant (Courant and Robbins, 1941) to unveil their power and beauty.

Looked at from a slightly different perspective, using Rena's terminology, what I had done was to make the questions around mathematics and education *real* for me. Five years and three degrees later I found myself as a mathematics teacher educator. My graduate school experience was almost the exact inverse of my undergraduate record. I cared deeply, worked hard and did well. Two of those five years were spent in England. There I was considerably influenced by the outlook and activities of the Association of Teachers of Mathematics. The leading members of the ATM combined a knowledge of, and love for, mathematics, with some deep insights into human psychology, a passion for learning in general and a respect for, and an enjoyment of, the world of children which I found highly attractive.

That influence turns out to have another dimension in this piece of work. As reports of Rena's numerous sabbatical activities began to filter back to her envious, snow-bound, memo-maddened friend and colleague, a constant refrain was that of 'I am so lucky to have found Eileen to work with; she is a wonderful teacher'. And as the samples of children's work grew more extensive and detailed I had to concede that, yet again, Dr U was spot on. It was quite some time later as I read an early draft of Eileen's part of this chapter that I realised, with a small, sharp thrill of 'of course!' recognition, that she too had been very influenced by the ATM. In her case it was through her contact with John Trivett who had been a leading member of the Association before coming to Vancouver.

And then Rena. You are about to get some insights into what she can bring out of children. It has been my privilege to have observed wondrous teaching acts with adolescents and adult learners as well. These episodes have a number of things in common. Perhaps the most important is authenticity. This is not to downplay the role of energy, intelligence, organisational ability, social skills, and enthusiasm, all of which Rena has in abundance.

It was a particularly able graduate student whose observation focused my attention on this aspect of Rena's teaching. 'You know, Rena never asks a student to do something that she does not do herself', was the comment, and it made me realise how rare a phenomenon this is in educational settings. 'Maths is fun', the teacher tells his class. Yet every other clue points to the reality that he would rather lick rat poison than have anything to do with equations in his spare time.

In concluding these introductory remarks, let me make a final observation while some element of my 'external' status remains. I believe that the work which Eileen and Rena and their young co-workers have done is of critical importance, not just for the teaching of mathematics, but also for the very active, wider debate concerning priorities for, and approaches to, public education.

One aspect of the discipline of mathematics which is of special importance to its devotees is that of 'proof'. More than with any other humanly-constructed artifact, there is, once certain logical criteria have been met, a sense of sureness in mathematics. Something *must be the case* or equivalently, *must be true*, because *we have proved it*. Among other things, a proof allows us to see *why*. The logician Iu Manin (1977, p. 51) has remarked: 'A good proof is one which makes us wiser'.

The methods of proof are numerous, diverse and ingenious. It is significant in the context of this work that the language of judgement around the concept of proof is very largely aesthetic. In this range of approaches there is a category known as proof by existence. We know that it is possible to have objects of a certain type because an instance has been produced.

In a fundamental sense what we have with Rena and Eileen's work is a 'proof by existence' of the possibility of a different and powerful way of approaching elementary school mathematics. Their methods have many features in common with the more widely known contemporary approaches to reform in mathematics education, especially those outlined in the 'Standards' documents for Curriculum and Evalutaion, for Professional Practice, and for Assessment generated by the American National Council of Teachers of Mathematics (NCTM, 1989, 1991, 1995).

Both approaches argue for more active and involved pupils, for materials-rich classrooms characterised by strong connections to the 'real world', and for co-operative and collaborative methodologies. Both approaches are based on an awareness that the classical patterns of mathematics teaching lead directly to the unquestioning acceptance of authority and its concomitant loss of meaning. 'Sit down, shut up and do what you are told' has been the operating structure for all too many mathematics classes. It should not come as a surprise that the response of learners to this approach has very often been confusion, frustration, hostility, and a strongly negative attitude toward any enterprise involving maths.

A widespread antipathy to mathematics might not be of particular importance except for the fact that the contemporary world is, for better or for worse, very largely, and increasingly, a mathematised one. To be porridge- or opera-avoidant is not to circumscribe one's world in any major way. To separate oneself from contexts that are mathematical is, however, to limit dramatically the range of one's options in the world.

This leaves us with a set of major problems that I will pose in a conventional academic way. Consider the following claims (which are basically restatements of arguments made above):

(a) to participate fully in the modern world (as informed citizen, employable individual, etc.), one needs to be mathematically fluent – or perhaps more accurately, and to show an example of how pervasive these concepts are – the probability of one's being able to participate fully in the contemporary world varies in direct relation to one's level of mathematical competence;

(b) mathematical fluency has traditionally been acquired at the cost of accepting an approach to learning and knowledge which accentuates separation, abstraction, the acceptance of authority, and a sharp distinction between 'right' and 'wrong';

(c) the contemporary world is highly mathematised;

(d) the contemporary world is fraught with manifold dangers, from the hazards of pollution, and overpopulation, to the nuclear risk and the growing prevalence of localised violence.

Starting from the four claims listed above, the following questions are among those that can be asked:

(1) What is the connection, if any, between (c) and (d)?

(2) What is the relationship between (b) and (c) and (b) and (d)?

(3) If one accepts (a), are there alternatives to (b)?

(4) Bonus Question: What are the possible implications of question (3) for (c), (d), and (b)?

These are non-trivial questions. Without going into detail, let me state that the essence of my answers to (1) and (2) would be of the order of: 'the connections are numerous and strong'. In a sense, this whole book is a combined, positive, response to question (3). Our claim is that alternatives exist. Eileen and Rena's contributions will outline the way in which one alternative methodology, a constructive-aesthetic approach, has worked in one classroom. My role will be to comment from a distance, particularly on the mathematical aspects of this work. Rena's and Eileen's descriptions speak forcefully and convincingly about the social, integrative, and pedagogical potential of their approach. My challenge will be to argue for the mathematical merits of working with children in this way.

In our discussions about the approach we wanted to take to this work, there was a strong consensus that we wished to write in a style that was personal and direct. In choosing to write invitationally, and in attempting to avoid the pomposity and jargon that characterises far too much of the literature of education, our ambition was to make something that interests, stimulates and supports those individuals attracted to a certain type of teaching and learning. This book is intended, therefore, for teachers, parents, and other educators, who are caring, seeking, imaginative, open and intelligent; individuals who might well feel, in some imprecise way, that more might be made of the teaching of mathematics.

Chapter 2

Tessellations

'No floor showing'

RENA

'So just what is a tessellation?' This was a popular question as I began to talk about the tessellations project to colleagues and friends. Well, a 'grown-up mathematician's' definition of tessellations might run something like this: tessellations or tilings are patterns of geometric figures that 'fit together perfectly to cover a flat surface . . . [so that] the pieces cover the plane without overlapping one another or leaving any gaps' (Peterson, 1990, pp. 72–3). The mathematician might add that tessellating patterns have been used by artists world-wide for centuries, in designing carpets, mosaics, fabrics and buildings.

Many people find the study of tessellations compelling. As Peterson claims, while tessellations have 'seemingly childish ingredients', the mathematical problems raised by working with tessellations are difficult, and even partial answers to those problems provide tools for 'exploring the frontiers of mathematics' (p. 73).

According to the children, however, the definition for tessellations was much simpler: 'Tessellations are where there is no floor showing'. When pressed further, the children could identify many other rules of tessellating patterns – 'there is no overlapping of shapes', and 'all quadrilaterals will tessellate', and so on. But I am getting ahead of myself.

I am not quite sure why we started with tessellations as the first maths project. Perhaps it was because I had already worked with tiled floor patterns for music composition. Maybe it was because Bill and I had talked a bit about tessellations the summer before this venture began, and I had a glimmering of how rich the explorations in this area of mathematics could be. Perhaps it was because I felt that I could bluff through the mathematics of tessellations (how complicated can a few polygons be?), and, I suppose, because tessellations were not a standard component of the Grade 3 and 4 curriculum. Or maybe it was simply because I knew there were some warehouse stores selling tiles not far from where I lived.

At any rate, I thought some nice ceramic tiles would make for a good beginning – they came in many colours and sizes. And while the shapes were limited to squares and the odd rectangle, I expected that there was still a good deal we could explore with simple shapes. Besides, the tiles looked beautiful and were smooth to the touch – as I mentioned in the opening chapter, aesthetically-pleasing materials are important to me.

Early explorations with tiles

So, in I came and (carefully) dumped tub-loads of ceramic tiles on the floor. The children dived in. I knew from past experiences that when working with new materials, it was best, at first, not to ask the children to do anything in particular – just let them go. After a while, they would be ready to try some suggestions I might make.

Not surprisingly, the suggestion I was ready to offer – 'try making a pattern with the tiles' – did not need to be made. Soon enough, the pupils were systematically attempting to create patterns, finding out which tiles fitted well together, and which did not (see Figure 2.1). Unlike kits of tessellating tiles or pattern blocks, not all of these tiles fitted conveniently together – the small tiles were either 1 inch or $1\frac{1}{8}$ inches square, while the larger ones ranged from $1\frac{1}{2}$ inches to 6 inches square. Thus, while each tile

Figure 2.1 Experimenting with tiles

could fit with other tiles in certain combinations, it was not the case that one side of each tile *would* necessarily fit with another particular tile. The children quickly discovered which tiles could be combined, and made a variety of tessellating patterns. At one point, I suggested they join with a partner if they would like to work on a pattern together. As a result, some children worked in pairs; others worked on their own.

Hardeep and Doug created what might best be termed a symmetrical structure rather than a tessellating pattern. As Doug said: 'It looks like a building'. As they glanced around them, and saw that others had created patterns qualitatively different from theirs, Hardeep became visibly concerned. I am sure he was worried that I was going to ask him to dismantle their work and do the 'assignment'. As I roamed over to see what they were making, Hardeep quickly piped up: 'It is not necessarily a pattern, but it is symmetrical'. I then asked him why it was not a pattern, to which he replied: ''Cause you would need at least a few more of them', meaning that their building could be part of a pattern of many buildings that were structured in the same way and fitted together.

Once the children had created a pattern to their liking, I asked them to 'write something down so that you can remember it or maybe show it to a friend'. This approach for encouraging children to develop their own notations for their tessellations is essentially the same approach I have used for years in teaching music composition through children's invented notations. That is, children are given the materials and time to create something that they like – something that has aesthetic appeal to the eye, to the ear, or to the touch. They are then invited to extend the experience in some way – by writing it down (as in this case), by taping it, by dramatising it, or, in some other form, by representing it in a new way and sharing it with others. It is through this extension that further learning can take place; as teachers are well aware, understanding something for oneself is one thing, but finding a way to relate it to others is something else again.

Notating tessellations

As soon as the children completed their notations of their patterns, I asked them to mix up the tiles and give their notations to someone else to see if their patterns could be recreated from the notations. I joined in this process, trying several of their notations, marvelling at the variety and complexity.

I read Andrea's notation first (see Figure 2.2). Her notation was impressive – a combination of words and arrows, centred around a single line. However, it was possible to misinterpret her original notation, and I read it incorrectly. She was quick to realise how her notation could be misinterpreted, and commented: 'Oh! I have an idea how I can change it.' When she showed her revised notation to Tanya, Andrea was obviously delighted that Tanya could interpret her notation and recreate the tile pattern.

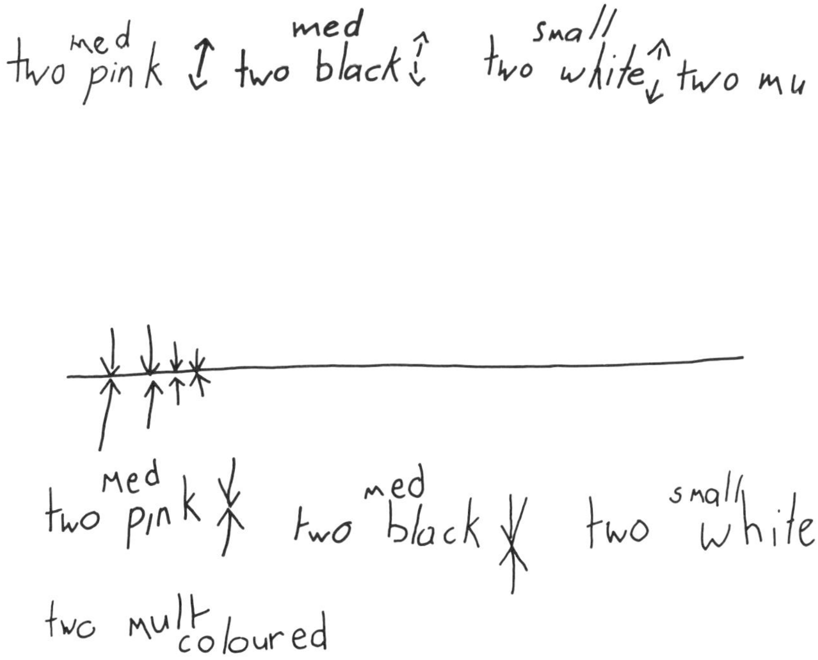

two ^med pink ↧ two ^med black ↥ two ^small white ↥ two mu

two ^med pink ↯ two ^med black ✗ two ^small white

two multi coloured

Figure 2.2 Two attempts at notating a tessellating pattern

I tried Hardeep's and Doug's notation next. Their building structure was exceedingly complex, and their notation was a one-to-one mapping of the structure – a picture of the structure with each tile drawn but not labelled by colour. While the configuration of the tiles was clear, I had trouble understanding which tiles were to be used. When I finished making the structure from the notation, Hardeep told me that I 'did a pretty good job', although it was clear that my interpretation was somehow lacking. Later, Stephanie worked from the same notation, and did a much better job. I commented on this to Hardeep, and he said with a shy smile (can a pupil be better than the teacher?): 'Actually, yes'.

For the second notation activity, I asked that the children use only two colours of the smallest squares to create a tessellating pattern. (By this point, I was using the words 'tessellate', 'tessellating' and 'tessellation' freely – I expected that by using them in context, the children would soon learn their meaning.) I also took part, by making both a pattern and a notation. Doug was visibly surprised: 'Are you making one too? Your own?' I answered: 'Yup, 'cause I never got to do one last time'. Children are often amazed when the teacher does the activity alongside them, but I was just as eager as they to play with the tiles.

This time Hardeep was determined to create a pattern of the kind that I had in mind, but, in what I was quickly learning to be 'true Hardeep style', he would try and make it by his rules as well as by mine. Hardeep was quite captivated by reflective symmetry, and proudly stated, while pointing to the tiles; 'Mine is a pattern *and* symmetrical. ... You can look at the pattern like that – black, white, black, white, but at the same time, there are two whites there, two blacks there and it is symmetrical somewhere around the middle of the tile.' In other words, Hardeep had found two lines of reflective symmetry (one horizontal and one vertical) for his tessellating pattern.

Andrea's pattern was quite complex, and I asked her to extend the tessellation so we could be sure of the pattern. Andrea beavered away at this task, and then noticed: 'You could actually fill the whole room with this pattern' – the logical extension of the 'no floor showing' idea.

It was not surprising to me that most children found it relatively simple to notate patterns using only the two types of tiles. Tracey commented: 'These are pretty easy.' When asked why, Doug answered: 'Only two colours', and Stephanie stated: 'Only one size.' If the tessellation is a simple one, the notation needed to describe it also tends to be rather unsophisticated. This did not come as a surprise to me either, given children's ways of notating common melodies.

When children are given a melody that is as well known to them as it is to others, they usually notate the melody in a very simple way. For example, to notate *Twinkle, Twinkle, Little Star*, children may only draw a few stars, claiming that their friends would be able to recognise the song because '*anyone* would know that's supposed to be *Twinkle, Twinkle, Little Star*' (Upitis, 1990b, p. 95).

This was also the case for tessellations. When the tessellating pattern was a simple one, children found it easiest to notate the pattern by drawing a replica of their design – like Hardeep's drawing of his pattern that was both tessellating and symmetrical (see Figure 2.3).

(a) Original pattern

Figure 2.3 Hardeep's notation

(b) Child's notation (of his own pattern)

On the other hand, when the pattern was more complex, children invented
a number of systems to record the information (see Figure 2.4).

Figure 2.4 (a) The original pattern; (b)–(g) Some children's notations for it

White brown brown repeat
downwards, and each
time shift to the
right

(b)

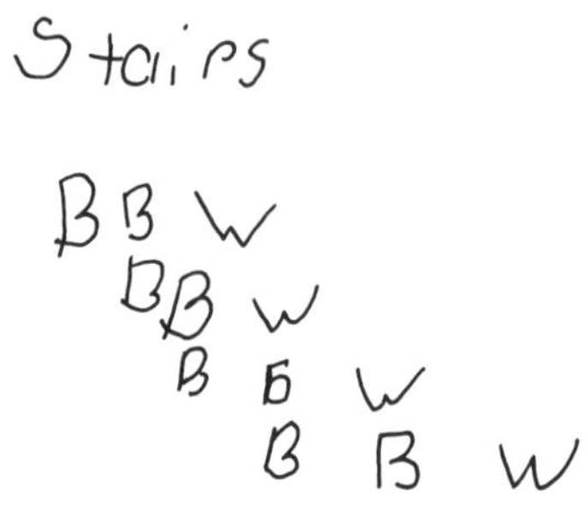

Stairs

B B W
 B B W
  B Б W
   B B W

(c)

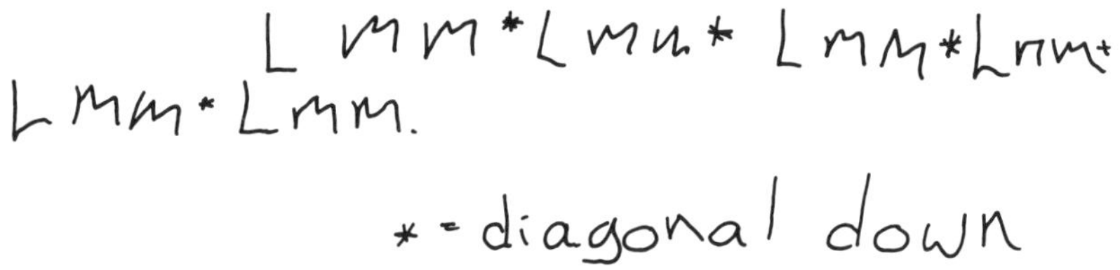

L мм * L мм * L мм * L пм
L мм * L мм.

*= diagonal down

(d)

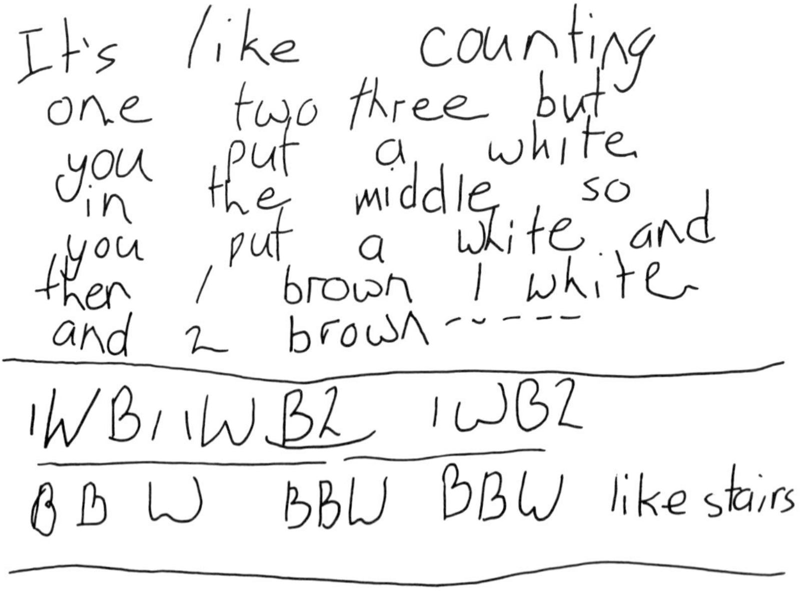

It's like   counting
 one   two three but
 you   put   a   white
  in   the   middle   so
 you   put   a   white and
 then / brown I white
 and 2   brown ~~---

IW B/ IW B2   IW B2
B B W   BBW BBW like stairs

(e)

$$3\left(\begin{array}{c}3\times3 \ square \\ alltenate \ B\backslash W \\ \rightarrow \ \ 1\square\end{array}\right)$$

(f)

White   Multi Colored

White — W   MC multi color

W MC W MC MC W MC MC MC W MC MC
MC MC W MC MC MC MC MC MC

W B (B+1)

(g)

While the number of notations I collected from the children were too few to make any generalisations about children's notations of tessellations, it would appear that the methods used for notating tessellations are as varied as those used by children of the same age when notating music compositions. In both cases, children use strings of numbers or letters, words, mathematical symbols and operations, icons, and placement on the page.

Walking through the world with a tessellating lens

I am confident that children are understanding something deeply when they make casual observations indicating that the phenomenon under study is being used to enrich their ways of walking through their worlds. Early on, Tanya came bursting into the room saying: 'When I went to McDonald's last night, there was a tessellation on the ceiling!' Before I had a chance to ask her what kind of pattern she had seen on the ceiling, others in the group offered their own examples. Their observations spilled from their mouths – this was not a slow and painful searching for possibilities. They had obviously seen so many examples of tessellations that they could describe them readily and in considerable detail – tessellating sidewalks, walls in shopping malls, and kitchen counters.

Hardeep plunged in with a description of his observations of bathroom tiles:

> It was in my uncle's house; it was the same kind of tiles I have at home, but it was a better colour. Blue. It was square, but in the one corner it just had a flower, about four or five petals. And it was blue.

The tessellations lingo soon spread to the Grade 4 pupils. One of the Grade 4 children in the class was from Iran. When she described the maths project on tessellations to her mother, her mother told her that rug makers know all about tessellations, since their knowledge of such patterns is used to create the intricate designs on Persian rugs. Rishma arrived with her mother's book of Persian rug illustrations, not only of the finished rugs themselves, but of the sketches of the tessellating patterns used to create the rugs. The children clamoured to see the book (see Figure 2.5). I almost think they were more interested in the mathematical sketches and painted grid drawings than in the photographs of the completed rugs. I would venture to conjecture that the opposite would have been true before this project began.

Meanwhile, tessellations were also becoming a part of my world. At the time that we were exploring tessellations, I was part-way through an elementary pottery course. While Tanya was gazing at ceilings in McDonald's, and Hardeep was comparing his uncle's tiles with his own, I was trying to vary my designs and glazes. Ideas for glazing were slow in coming until I realised that I could use a tessellating pattern on the bottom of a plate or a bowl; I spent many an hour designing square tiles to tessellate over the outside surface of my pasta bowls. I came in one morning with several sketches in hand and proudly showed them to my teacher. She was

(a)

Figure 2.5 Persian rug tessellations

(b)

pleased, but complicated the picture by asking how I was planning to adjust the pattern for the curved sides of the bowl.

Tessellations on curved surfaces? Perhaps I was getting a bit ahead of myself once again. I rang up Bill for advice. Undaunted, Bill gave me a reference on just this issue. I could learn how to put a tessellating pattern on an egg – a formidable curved surface – if I spent a little time reading 'Adventures of an Egg Man', where Paul Hoffman (1988) describes how the citizens of Vegreville, Alberta learned just how difficult it was to create a three-and-a-half-storey Ukrainian Easter egg. I preferred my pottery teacher's more pragmatic solution. She suggested I make a transparency of the pattern and project it onto the bowl using an overhead projector, and then trace the projected image directly onto the surface of the bowl. An ingenious solution.

I am convinced that one of the reasons that the children began to see tessellating patterns they would have otherwise overlooked is that they recognised the mathematics in the patterns, and worked with it. The children did more than recognise tessellations at McDonald's. They examined the tessellations, and asked themselves questions like: 'Is it made from quadrilaterals and triangles, or from some other polygons that sometimes tessellate?' In contrast, so much of the traditional geometry curriculum is concerned with 'recognising shapes' not doing something with them.

The McDonald's episode and the Persian rugs story are two examples in which children identified tessellations without prompting on my part. But once it was clear that they were, in fact, 'seeing' tessellations, I asked them to bring in examples of tessellating patterns from outside the classroom, suggesting that they look through some magazines and clip out some photographs. This request yielded a rich variety of examples. Tracey offered one of hers first, a photograph of a tiled roof. With a twinkle in her eye, she pointed out that: 'no holes is even more important for a roof than a floor'. Others offered examples of rugs and bathroom tiles, fabric samples and Italian walkways.

Developing a description of the characteristics of tessellations

A few weeks after the project began, I overheard one of the children ask: 'What's tessellate again?', to which another answered: 'So you don't see the floor'. I am sure that the child who asked the question knew very well how to work with and describe a tessellation. I think she was looking for another definition, someone else's words, to make her understanding fuller. For several weeks, the children were engaged in this kind of talk as they explored tessellations more deeply.

One of the first characteristics of tessellations articulated by the children was that 'most quadrilaterals tessellate'. In fact, *all* quadrilaterals tessellate (a claim I will come back to in the final chapter), but the children were unwilling to make such a statement for some time. Similarly, all triangles tessellate, but again it took a while before they were convinced of this.

The children's understanding of the 'rules' of tessellations started with the knowledge that squares would tessellate. This was clear from the beginning, and I am sure that they were aware of this even before working with the ceramic tiles. It was from here that I began to probe further, beginning with a question: 'What other shapes will tessellate besides squares, do you think?'

Hardeep answered: 'Triangles will, 'cause all you have to do is flip it over for a square.'

And Doug quickly added: 'Rectangles too.'

And Tracey: 'And hexagons.'

And Stephanie: 'I saw one that was a diamond.'

And Jon: 'Miss Upitis! Rectangles tessellate!'

And finally, Sam: 'All squares tessellate, huh?'

Soon after, I gave the children several different triangle types cut from different colours of construction paper (right-angled, equilateral, isosceles, and scalene), and asked them if they could make the triangles tessellate. They became quite engrossed in this, muttering to themselves every once in a while, 'How can I make it?', 'Oh, I see how ... wait a minute, ... no. Maybe this!'

Tanya made quite a lovely tessellation with different colours of right-angled triangles, and the group was excited by her discovery – when I listened later to the tape of the session, there was a dramatic hush followed by silence as the children viewed her work. Andrea broke the silence: 'Wow! That's a nice one. I would have never thought of that one.' I took advantage of their attention. Since I wanted them to begin considering slide transformations (or transposition in the music lingo; see Chapter 5), I asked: 'What happens if you just shove one row somewhere?' After I moved one row of Tanya's pattern, Erika whispered: 'Oh, wow'.

Working with square tiles and dot grids

One book that I made use of during this project was called *Introduction to Tessellations*, by Dale Seymour and Jill Britton (1989). It is a wonderful book – and yes, I learned about it from Bill. The book contains hundreds of examples of tessellating patterns, many of which are simple combinations of unusual quadrilaterals yielding elegant designs. There are also many illustrations of Escher paintings, and methods for creating 'Escher-like' tessellations are outlined. The children were fascinated by a tessellation of dogs, because they could see how a simple square was transformed into a dog, which could then be tessellated over the page.

Another feature of the book is that a series of dot-grid pages is provided, all of which can be photocopied so that people can make their own tessellating patterns on paper. Having spent a considerable amount of time manipulating objects and searching for tessellations inside and outside the classroom, I was sure that giving the children a couple of different kinds of dot-grids would yield some interesting results. Andrea created a pattern of arrows, a tessellation that, in fact, appears in the Seymour and Britton book (see Figure 2.6). Jon made a number of tessellations from triangles and, like many of the other children, coloured the tessellating patterns. I had not asked the children to colour their tessellations, but the extra care that the colouring took not only indicated their investment in their work, but highlighted the beauty of the tessellations as well.

One of the most important outcomes of the dot-grid pages was discovering a polygon that *would not* tessellate. Doug had drawn two octagons next to each other, and written 'ECT' [*et cetera*] beside it, indicating his belief that the octagon would tessellate. I asked if any others shared Doug's view. Some did; others did not. But no one was firmly committed one way or another. I extended Doug's drawing, and it became obvious to everyone that the octagons would not tessellate.

Hardeep was most troubled by this result, stating that it did not make sense since 'octagons are really double quadrilaterals'. Stephanie followed up with the comment, 'Yeah, but three-sided ones work', almost as if, in the face of learning about a polygon that would not tessellate, she needed to reaffirm her understanding of polygons that did. The following week, I drew for Doug a tessellating pattern of octagons and squares that I had seen on the sidewalk down the street from where I lived. This made a big impression on him; he would often refer to this example as: 'a way Miss Upitis found you could make an octagon tessellate'.

By this time, the children's fascination with unusual tessellations had reached a peak. When I was telling Bill about our work to this point, he sent me a pattern of tessellating pentagons (see Figure 2.7) that he had just produced. Andrea's theory was that the tessellation worked because the

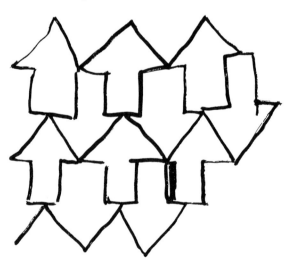

Figure 2.6 Andrea's arrows

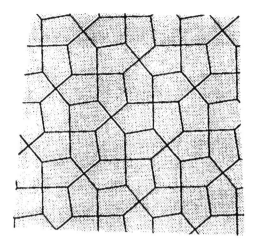

Figure 2.7 Tessellating pentagons

pattern was really 'stretched hexagons laid over each other'. Everyone wanted the pattern for their notebooks, where they had been madly pasting in interesting tessellation examples. So I obliged, chopping Bill's lovely page into a dozen pieces (I kept one for my notebook too).

The children continued to come up with more examples of tessellations in the 'outside world'. Someone pointed out that there was a tessellation on Doug's shirt one day, a picture of soccer balls (tessellating pentagons again). I realised later that this was a pretty special case, because all of the pentagons end up covering a spherical three-dimensional (3-D) surface – and I thought about the possible connections between soccer balls and pasta bowls.

The final tessellation exploration we undertook was the creation of square tiles, each of which were decorated with a pattern. The patterns were created by joining dots that cut each side of the square into thirds, so that no matter how the tiles were assembled, an interesting design would result (see Figure 2.8). I

Figure 2.8 Single square tile

(a)

Figure 2.9 Two different 3 × 3 arrangements of the original square tile

used these tiles to work further with transformations, showing the children how I could change my pattern by applying a 'rule for changing the way that the squares are oriented' (see Figure 2.9). The children created their own tiles, suggested rules to one another, and then manipulated the tiles accordingly.

When I asked them to find a way to write down their patterns and their rules, they baulked. Andrea commented: 'Oh wow, that's going to be hard', and tried to notate her pattern. But the next day, she could not recreate the tiling, commenting: 'I can't find the exact one. I should have written something on the back, like no. 1 bottom'. Developing a notation for transformations like rotations was a bit too sophisticated at this point. But the children had an amazing amount of knowledge about tessellations nonetheless, and many a pattern to use as we embarked on the silk painting adventure.

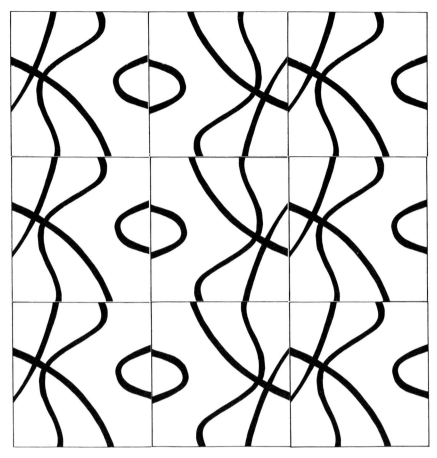

(b)

Tessellations on silk

Five weeks into the project, Eileen and I began planning a joint Grade 3 and 4 enterprise which involved making greeting cards by painting tessellating patterns on silk. Eileen was planning to use pattern blocks with the Grade 4 pupils for their first informal encounter with tessellations, so I too brought pattern blocks into the Grade 3 arena.

Many teachers will be familiar with pattern blocks – plastic or wooden polygons made up of a number of shapes and colours, including equilateral triangles, trapezoids, parallelograms, squares, regular hexagons, and so on. Further, the sides of each polygon correspond in length to at least one other polygon (for example, the side of the regular hexagon is the same length as the side of the equilateral triangle as well as the shortest side of the trapezoid).

When I first pulled out the pattern blocks, the children were delighted to play with the blocks with their new knowledge of tessellations, commenting: 'We had these in Grade 2, but I didn't know what you could do then.' After a relatively short while, however, some frustrations began to surface. Manufacturers of pattern blocks design them so that most are 'guaranteed' to tessellate – each shape tessellates on its own, and since the sides of the various shapes are also co-ordinated, many of the shapes tessellate with each other. These children, however, were quite disappointed by the limited choices, saying: 'Oh! Hexagons! And diamonds! Are there any octagons? Oh no. . . . These are boring 'cause you know they all tessellate.'

Boring the pattern blocks might have been, but they nonetheless gave the children a number of new ideas for their silk designs. When the time came to design their cards, they were free to use any tessellating patterns – from the ceramic tiles, from their dot-grid patterns, from the square tiles they designed themselves, or from any other source. Many, in fact, used the pattern blocks in the last analysis, since it was simpler to trace a block than to draw a less predictable polygon freehand.

Jon asked if he could use circles. When I asked the others if circles would tessellate, many quickly replied that they would, but with a moment's reflection, began to question their immediate response: 'Can circles? With tiny diamonds in the corners? Oh no, it wouldn't work because there would be a little straight part on the side.' They realised, ultimately, that circles could not tessellate.

Around this time, Eileen and I stayed after school one day and made our own silk cards. While we were painting, we discussed how the Grade 4 pupils could get a 'crash course' on tessellations so that they could successfully take part in the project. Eileen came up with the idea of having the Grade 3 children act as a panel of experts on tessellations, relating what they knew to their Grade 4 classmates. The 'Grade 3 Panel of Experts' class was one that Eileen would lead, following her introductory work on tessellations using the pattern blocks with the Grade 4 pupils.

The days that Eileen led the class in open explorations of tessellations (during 'regular' maths classes) gave me the privileged opportunity of watching Eileen's expert mediation and considerable teaching skill. In just two classes, she not only teased out the Grade 3 pupils' knowledge of tessellations, but helped them articulate it to the Grade 4 pupils, related it to work that the class had done a month earlier on tangrams, taught a quick lesson on colour mixing (we had only the primary colours for silk painting), and had all of the pupils creating several rough sketches of tessellating patterns they might use on their cards.

By the end of the first day, the Grade 3 and 4 pupils had established these characteristics and 'rules' about tessellations:

- they make a pattern with shapes, with no space or overlapping;
- they use shapes like triangles and quadrilaterals;
- all triangles, quadrilaterals, and even some hexagons tessellate;
- other shapes can tessellate if you combine them with squares and triangles, like an octagon with a diamond;
- you can make patterns on a shape that tessellates (with the corollary that 'if you make a pattern or design with shapes on a hexagon, it is not a tessellation unless the whole hexagon tessellates too');
- you have to use shapes with straight sides.

When asked to think of some hints that would help make the tessellations easier to design, the Grade 3 children came up with the following:

- keep it simple;
- use only one or two shapes;
- make sure the pattern repeats, and do not make a maze or something else that is not a tessellation;
- cover the paper;
- no overlapping of shapes is allowed.

At this point, Eileen invited the children to try their own rough sketches. Each child took a piece of newsprint and folded it in eighths, filling each of the resulting squares with a different pattern. Some beautiful tessellations were created, with and without the help of the pattern blocks.

A lovely incident occurred around Doug's work as he was creating his fourth or fifth pattern; he happened to create a tessellation with diamonds that excited him as well as everyone around him because it gave the illusion of a 3-D pattern. He wrote on his paper, with great pride: 'I discoverded it.' When I came to his table, he told me: 'and I let Jennifer use it. And Scott's using my other one.' I then told Doug, and all of the children within earshot, that I had just read about Marjorie Rice, who had discovered a new tessellating polygon in 1974 (Peterson, 1990).

The children were visibly impressed, not only because the discovery was a recent one, but because it meant that they might also discover a tessellation new to the world. And Rishma exclaimed, 'Yeah! A woman, even!' – here is at least one girl who is unlikely to buy into the 'Math[s] class is tough' Barbie myth. Of course, Doug asked if anyone had discovered his particular pattern before, and I had to tell him that, indeed, he was not the first to tessellate this particular quadrilateral. He was not disappointed; the possibility of being the first to discover another tessellation still remained.

The following day, Doug's 'diamond tessellation' had spread around the room. He added his own version of a registered trademark symbol to his sketch (see Figure 2.10), and told me: 'I could have sold this – for five bucks!'

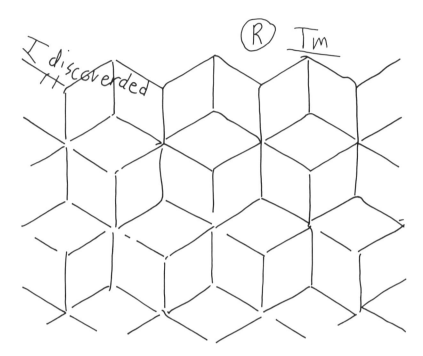

Figure 2.10 Evidence of Doug's pride in his discovery of a tessellating pattern

No doubt. In a class discussion later that day, he pointed out how many people were using his tessellation, and while he was happy to have it shared, he wanted to be sure that everyone knew that he had discovered it – at least in this classroom – *first*. As educators, we would like children to learn about spelling and rules of grammar by becoming writers; we would like children to learn about music theory and performance by becoming composers; we would like children to learn about arithmetic and concepts of mathematics by becoming mathematicians – makers of mathematics. Doug had surely become a mathematician, for a couple of classes at least.

When Eileen gathered the pupils to the carpet at the end of the day, she invited them all to share any new thoughts they might have about tessellations.

Someone immediately offered: 'You can make 3-D with tessellations.'

To which Doug piped up: 'Yeah, I'm the one that discovered that!'

Another Grade 4 pupil noted: 'They're only tessellations if they cover the whole paper.'

Hardeep modified the latter observation:

Well, actually, a tessellation does not necessarily have to cover the whole page. The Grade 3s, and me too, thought it did, but really, all you have to do is make it go 2 or 3 times around. Like the first day Miss Upitis came and we made tiles on the floor, we didn't cover the whole floor or anything. It's just till you see the pattern.

When Eileen drew a trapezoid on the board and asked for comments, another rich flow of information came forth.

'You could put another one of those and make like a double – a hexagon.'
'It has three triangles in it too, or a diamond and a triangle.'
'If you make two right-angled triangles on it you can make a rectangle.'

I followed Eileen's cue by drawing a pentagon on the board – a form of pentagon that tessellates (many of them do not), and asked the children if it would tessellate. They confidently answered that it would: 'because you can see how the triangle and square fit with each other'. Pentagons, Bill tells me, are a special case. Apparently much is known about properties of tiles with four or fewer sides, and similarly of tiles with six or more sides. However, there may be new combinations of tessellating pentagons that have yet to be discovered. While I know from our conversations that he would have liked me to have 'pushed the work with pentagons further', I did not – partly because we already had enough to work with, and partly because I was not sure how.

With a few parent volunteers and a couple of extra irons, we were ready to spend most of the afternoon making our silk cards. Using the same process that was described in Rishma's book on Persian rugs, we had made our rough sketches and our accurate drawings, and were then ready to work with the medium – in this case, painting on silk fabric. But before I describe the process, here is a list of the materials we used:

- water soluble, non-toxic fabric paint;
- silk resist;
- silk (cut in pieces approximately 12 cm × 17 cm);
- water for diluting paint and cleaning brushes;
- fine paint brushes;
- felt pens and/or pencil crayons;
- masking tape;
- a greeting card with a window for each child (approximately 10 cm × 15 cm) made from stiff recycled card stock;
- a second card, of the same size, without a window;
- a rectangular piece of card, cut slightly smaller than the silk, but larger than the window;
- envelopes (preferably recycled stock);
- paper towels;
- iron and surface for ironing;
- tub with water;
- artists' spray glue.

The children were invited to draw their favourite tessellation on the second greeting card: that is, the greeting card without the window. Some of them drew their tessellations with pencil crayon, others with thin black felt pens (see Figure 2.11).

Figure 2.11 Designing patterns for silk cards

When their drawing was complete, they taped a piece of silk on the card, so that the four corners were secured, and so that the pattern would be visible through the silk.

Following this, they traced their tessellation with silk resist. Once the resist had dried, they painted their tessellation, according to the colour scheme they had decided on earlier. In some cases, there was a bit of 'leaking' through the resist, but this was not cause for alarm as the results were still pleasing – a bit like painting wet-into-wet in watercolours. This process took about three-quarters of an hour; heads were bent in silent concentration as the children meticulously applied the resist and painted the silk.

Once the silk was painted, it was plied away from the card and rinsed in a tub of water to remove most of the resist (see Figure 2.12). Many of the children were somewhat dismayed as the rinsing caused some of the paint to run off as well; they were assured that paint ran off my card as well as Eileen's, and that all would be well. After the quick rinse, the silk was ironed between two pieces of paper towelling to 'fix' the colour onto the fabric (there were two ironing stations in the room – with parent volunteers rinsing and ironing).[4]

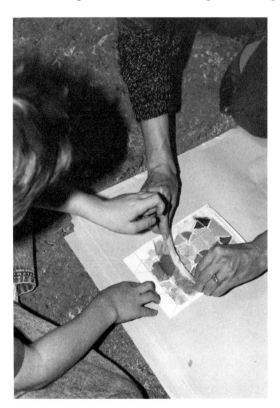

Figure 2.12 Removing silk from cardboard backing

The completed silk painting was then glued to the rectangular piece of card; the resulting 'insert' was glued to the window, and the children had two cards each to their credit. The first was the silk card, the second was the card 'left over' after the silk piece had been removed. This second 'left-over' card had the same pattern as the silk card, except that it was on card stock rather than fabric, and was outlined in pen or coloured pencil.

This was a fantastic activity, and caused great excitement amongst the children and adults in the room. The work was skilful and beautiful. Eileen and I were delighted to see that many of the cards created by the children were more appealing than our own. It was also interesting to note that Eileen and I, as well as the mothers who came in to help, found that the Grade 3 children generally produced better work than the Grade 4 children, even though they were a year younger and therefore potentially disadvantaged in terms of the fine-motor skills required for this kind of work. This activity certainly convinced me that the weeks of 'messing about with tessellations' the Grade 3s had experienced had made a tangible impact on them. As Eileen said that day after school, it helped 'put it in their gut' in a way that did not happen for the Grade 4 pupils.

I wish I had had a tape recorder running while the parents were working with the children. I managed to jot down a couple of the comments:

'I wish we had had maths like this when I was in school.'

'I had the best job. When I finished spraying the glue, and the children saw their silk on the card, their faces glowed. Just glowed.'

I wondered at the time whether any of these parents were the ones who had expressed concern over Eileen's maths curriculum – sometimes it is easier to understand something new when working along with children.

Of course, the pupils had their own ways of describing their work. One of my favourites was Andrea's gleeful burst, 'Miss Upitis! I tessellated trapezoids and triangles!' While Andrea and others were showing me their cards (see Figure 2.13), some of the other children were furiously writing away – these were real cards to be used to write letters to real people. Still others were copying down the brand names of the paint and resist, later asking me where they could purchase the supplies so that they could do this at home. If it is good enough to do at home, it must be real.

Perhaps the most gratifying part of the experience, for me, was to speak with several teachers after school. Three teachers came into Eileen's classroom a few moments after the bell rang, having seen the children walking down the hall with the cards, and wanting to know just how they had created them. One teacher, whom I had not met before, asked me if I was a 'maths person or an art person', and 'how much do you have to know about tessellations to do this'. (The word 'tessellation' had now spread through the school.) Eileen and I simultaneously answered 'maths', although later, we modified that to 'both'.

Figure 2.13 Showing off the card creations

The teachers stayed and talked and poured over the Seymour and Britton tessellations book for about 45 minutes – a long time for busy teachers to hang around 'just talking' after school. One of them said that there was nothing like this in their maths textbooks. (No kidding!) But this comment made me realise the difference between learning computational skills and mathematical patterns and concepts through a combination of manipulatives and textbook tasks, and our work described here.

What we were doing was extending the children's experience one step beyond learning with manipulatives. It makes lots of sense to have children learning about patterns and tessellations using tiles and pattern blocks and geoboards, or whatever. But it is something else again to *make* something from that knowledge, to craft something that is one's own. The children were interested in tessellations as a concept and learned a great deal using the manipulatives; they became even more eager to understand tessellations more fully when the possibility of creating something that was uniquely their own was presented. Suddenly, understandings good enough for 'maths purposes' (for example, that all quadrilaterals will tessellate) were pushed further – will *this* quadrilateral, this strangely-shaped, neither quite a diamond nor a parallelogram, tessellate?

I have noticed the same phenomenon when making silk tessellations with student teachers – learning the rules and concepts is one thing, using them is quite another. You can learn the rules with manipulatives (or with textbooks and worksheets), but you do not use the rules until you make something. I am convinced that when you *use* the rules, you learn them even better.

Making silk cards was significant enough to write about in journals as well. Several children, when writing about the tessellations project in their regular classroom journals, indicated how the project had gone beyond the school walls, and had become *real*:

> 'Well, my Mom thought it was fantastic. But she did not know it was silk until she touched it and thought it was excellent. I first was going to give it to my Dad but he said to give it to my Mom because she teaches grade one and she is always tired after school.'

> 'I liked the *silk* ones ... but to me, I love looking in our living room at the *carpet*. It *tessellates*.'

> 'I never showed my Mom because I am giving it to her for Christmas. It was neat when the paint went to the corners of the resist.'

> 'I loved doing tessellations ... it was very fun and it is nice cous [’cause] your [you’re] doing Maths and having fun while your doing it. My mom only got to see one the other one is the silk one and it's for Christmas. My sisters said how do you do that my dad said wow that's beautiful this is my dasine [design].'

I think it safe to say that this project was real for me, for Eileen, and for Bill as well. Before I steal all the thunder, I had better pass the pen.

EILEEN

From the moment Rena entered the room I knew I had made the right decision for my group. Her big blue bin of tiles was an instant hit. From my vantage point, I could hear the tiles clicking invitingly, and occasionally I caught glimpses of their sheening beauty. Pale by comparison were the strips of construction paper that my group was using to explore weaving patterns. Maybe there was something to Rena's belief that authentic materials should be used whenever possible.

The Grade 4's project, at this stage, involved weaving on a cardboard loom. They were using wool warp threads, but paper weft ones. Each pupil's task was to create a weaving that showed interesting patterns. To do this, they played around with changing both the warp and the weft weaving arrangements. Then they were to find ways to record what they had done enabling them to reproduce their pattern at a later date, or so someone else could reproduce it (the same form of instructions given to the Grade 3 children when they were notating their tessellations).

Many of them chose to write a type of code on their paper strips. For example:

wa 1lx11x   we   o2u1o2u1

meant:

> warp: wrap two threads, miss one, continue to end;
> weft: over 2, under 1, continue to end.

As soon as my group finished the first task: 'Find ways to record your [construction paper] weaving pattern so that someone else could reproduce it', I introduced wool for the weft as well. This added another dimension of 'real' material to their mathematical explorations. Weaving with wool added further complexity to the pupils' task. They became concerned with how much wool would be needed, how to join pieces, and how much tension to use. Two examples follow:

> 'Should I wrap it around the back, or loop it down onto the next row?'
> 'What do you think?'
> 'Well, if I wind it around the back, it'll take more wool. But if I loop it down, my pattern might not work … maybe I'll try and see.'

And:

> 'Help! Mine is curving in the middle!'
> 'Sometimes that is caused by too much tension.'
> 'Yeah, I think I pulled too hard. I want to put paper strips mixed in with my wool … it might keep it straighter.'

Pupils had to use estimation, prediction, trial and error, and planning strategies just to see if their weaving patterns would work. They devised ways to shuttle their wool back and forth. Some of them had to find solutions for uneven tension.

All pupils completed the project successfully. Some of the weavings were complex combinations of colour, texture, materials, and pattern, while others were simpler. The important thing was that each pupil experienced success, each pupil communicated mathematically to the group, and each pupil used mathematics to make something of personal value.

Not surprisingly, the two groups (Rena's and mine) were interested in each other's projects. The groups soon realised that it was acceptable to browse through the other group's work area. Tracey (one of the Grade 3s) became so intrigued with the weaving that she did one in her own time, gathering scraps from the trash and the recycling bin so that she would have enough wool and construction paper to create a pattern. Similarly, it was not long before the Grade 4s started using 'tessellating' vocabulary. It was great for me to see this informal exchange of information. Part of my job is to create opportunities for learning, give a bit of encouragement, and then watch, listen, and wait. This strategy certainly seemed to work here.

In a relaxed atmosphere, the children learned from each other, and both groups took pride in showing their discoveries. Meanwhile, I was also learning a great deal informally, and, like Rena and the Grade 3s, I was beginning to see tessellations everywhere. One day, I was on my way up the stairs to the staffroom after school to get us both a cup of tea, and I went running back into the classroom to tell Rena about the tessellating quadrilaterals on the rubber stair mats.

While Rena and I both believe that much is to be learned from informal exchanges, we also decided that the whole class should be more actively involved in each other's projects from time to time. The first instance of this was *Tessellations on Silk*, the greeting card project. I must admit I was a little nervous that the more experienced Grade 3s would badly outshine the Grade 4s. I did not want the Grade 4s to feel threatened or to be put into a situation where obvious comparisons could be made. In order to narrow the experience gap, Rena and I planned the 'panel of experts' strategy that she has described earlier in this chapter.

I took delight in watching and listening to the 'experts' relate their knowledge to their 'colleagues'. The Grade 3s knew their subject matter and the Grade 4s treated them with respect. Here is the panel, to provide a sense of the kinds of questions and comments the children made.

Doug was an extremely bright fellow who had a tendency to be a little anxious. He was so involved in the presentation that he spontaneously and very competently drew and described a complex tessellation on the board to illustrate a point he was making. The conversation between Doug, myself, and others follows:

Doug: If you are making a tessellation, and it is inside a shape, it will not be a tessellation unless the whole diagram is a shape that tessellates.

Rena: Oh! I know what you mean.

Eileen: I wish I understood that – can you do a sample on the board? I think you have to be really up on this to understand.

Doug: (while drawing a hexagon) Say you had this, and you are doing patterns in there [indicating the area inside the hexagon], the whole diagram is a shape, it is not tessellating, the whole outside has to tessellate. It is not a tessellation no matter what's inside, you have to put a lot more of them. It cannot be just one shape.

Eileen: O.K., so just filling the inside of the shape does not mean you've tessellated. You have to fill your whole paper – it is the outside shape that counts.

Rena: That is a bit like the tiles we made, 'cause the outside shape was a square, so no matter what squiggles you put on the tiles, you knew the squares would tessellate.

Eileen: The other question I have, and maybe the Grade 3s could help me with this, you said we could have two different shapes. Do all the

Doug:	shapes have to tessellate on their own? I can sorta give you an example [goes to board]. Well, if this was an octagon [draws octagon] and then another octagon [draws next to the first one, joined on one side], they will not tessellate unless you put a triangle.
Jon:	Not a triangle, a diamond.
Eileen:	Right, because if you look at a diamond shape, it is –
Andrea:	– two triangles.
Eileen:	So you are both right.

Stephanie and Tracey were still gaining fluency in English, their second language, and they too spoke effectively about the beauty of tessellations. Both of these girls were very capable at drawing, and they seemed to make the art/maths connection easily.

Erika, who could be rather difficult to 'hook' into a conversation, contributed voluntarily to the discussion.

Hardeep, an extremely gifted boy, with a dry wit and an extensive vocabulary, kept us all on track with his interjections: 'Well, actually, all quadrilaterals tessellate', and 'Not necessarily, you just need to develop a pattern until you can see it repeat'.

Andrea and Tanya shone with enthusiasm about every part of tessellations. These girls were deep thinkers and they internalised the patterns they made. They got so good at recording patterns that they could make representations on paper after viewing them only once.

Jon, who was just starting to show some of his potential at the time of this event, gave expert advice on keeping the patterns simple.

Sam, who could be a little embarrassed about having the spotlight, and who would often react in a 'silly' way to cover this, was very serious and sincere in his presentation. In fact, for most of the time that the Grade 3 panel stood at the front of the room facing the Grade 4 pupils, Sam acted as the mediating chairperson.

Jennifer was always eager, very bright, and extremely involved in everything around her. She was in her element.

It was still relatively early in the year when the Grade 3 expert panel was formed, and some of the Grade 3s were still feeling a little in awe of the Grade 4s. They were trying to be accepted as peers. They really put their whole hearts into this panel (learning by heart?). The Grade 4s were genuinely interested and impressed. They had a good idea of what the Grade 3s had been doing and they wanted to do it too. They asked questions and listened closely to the answers and opinions given.

I believe that one of the reasons my class operated so effectively for the rest of the year is because the 3s proved themselves to be so competent in this presentation. Since that time, the class acted as a mixed group, not as 3s separate from the 4s. Individuals often gave oral reports to the class, either voluntarily and informally (sharing journal entries or stories), or more formally, as part of a report or assignment. I noticed the attention and support the pupils gave each other. I have used the 'expert panel' as a group dynamics strategy several times since the year that Rena and I worked together.

Back to the tessellations. The day we made the cards was, as Rena said, exciting for everyone involved. Energy and a sense of purpose poured from each child. When Rena finished her brief explanation, all the children were fired up and ready to go. Even the 4s, less experienced with tessellations, seemed comfortable and confident. I have found that if children are not secure in what they are doing, they will ask questions forever. They will work at starting without actually beginning, and they will often want to change their initial idea, saying: 'I made a mistake'. We had none of this.

However, it was interesting that many of the parent volunteers were confused about the patterns of tessellations and the process the card-making would entail. Once again, the importance of understanding and hands-on experience was made clear to me. These parents were very capable helpers, but they needed guidance from the children, and from Rena and myself, to comprehend the nature of the desired product. They needed a learning chain that would take them from identification of tessellations, to manipulating shapes, to card creation. Words and sketches were not enough. As the children completed each step, it was the parents who were the most astonished at the project unfolding before them.

The children were, fittingly, extremely pleased and proud. They expected high quality results, and were not surprised to see high quality results emerge. I had already gone through my 'astonishment stage' a few days earlier when I viewed the class drawing their initial tessellations. But for the parents, each stage of the experience was new.

Because I did not have a sink in my classroom, it was necessary to have the pupils make several trips down the hall to use the sink in the janitor's closet. Other teachers became aware of the increased activity in room 108 and as soon as the dismissal bell rang, colleagues began to arrive at my door to see what was going on. One teacher, who had earlier told me that she felt maths was the easiest subject to evaluate because it was 'so black and white', finally agreed that perhaps there was room for alternative methods of assessment. Others had to be persuaded to see this type of project as 'mathematics as well as art'.

This led us to talk about the integration of subject matter in authentic ways. Rena commented: 'Everything starts out integrated, it is we [teachers] who have disintegrated it'. This has proven to be one of my favourite ideas to reflect upon. At the time, all present had a great discussion about the connotations of 'disintegration/dis-integration'.

Just before the winter break, almost a month after the silk cards were made, the entire class was making gingerbread houses. I had put some sample photos up to inspire the children and to help them decide what materials they wanted to use as decorations. I overheard some of them talking about the pros and cons of Smarties versus Shreddies as roofing material.

'Fine, you get Smarties and see how they melt and colour your hands! I am going to use Shreddies. They look real, and besides, they tessellate.'

The last thing I want to comment on relating to the tessellations project occurred several months later, when the class was working with geoboards. I have used geoboards for over 20 years to help clarify concepts of multiplication. I also use them to teach area, perimeter, fractions, and geometry concepts. During the introductory stages, I want to be sure that children can represent their geoboard patterns accurately on dotted paper (similar to the dot-grid paper used by the Grade 3s and described by Rena earlier). This usually involves a lot of practice. Pupils often have difficulty identifying where their geoboard peg is on the dotted paper. They sometimes create shapes that they cannot reproduce and have to be encouraged to start with a simpler design. Pupils usually have difficulty with oral descriptions because a new vocabulary has to be learned.

This group was quite different. While they worked, I encouraged them to talk about what they were doing. The vocabulary of plane figures came naturally to most of them. I am sure this was because of their previous experience with the language of tessellations. Nevertheless, I was thrilled with their recall. After all, it had been three months since we had made our greeting cards, quite a long while in a young pupil's life. I heard comments like:

'I made a trapezoid first, and then I turned it into a hexagon.'

'I used triangles and rectangles to make these pentagons.'

When I was looking over the papers at the end of the day, I was impressed by the complexity of the shapes and with the accuracy of the transpositions (see Figure 2.14). Their previous experience at manipulating and drawing their tessellations had obviously stayed with them and transferred to this new context. Their work with geoboards was superior to the work of any other group I had taught. Patterns that had been used for tessellations had been adapted to geoboards. This, in itself, is quite exciting since transfer is often difficult to achieve from one context to another. It is even more impressive considering the time that had elapsed since the tessellation explorations.

Tessellations were obviously real – really powerful, really useful, really adaptable.

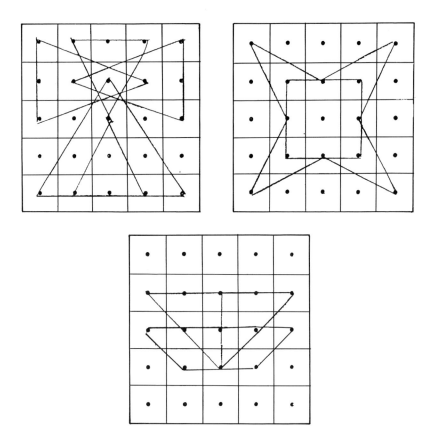

Figure 2.14 Geoboard patterns

BILL

The theme of tessellations is a somewhat odd one in the elementary school curriculum. Not often made compulsory as a central topic, it nevertheless appears relatively frequently as an application or enrichment unit at different grade levels. There are several reasons for this. First, it is a topic which fits the general curriculum emphases, particularly in geometry, quite well. Take, for example, the American NCTM Standard 9 at the K-4 level for geometry and spatial sense, which states that:

> In grades K-4, the mathematics curriculum should include two- and three-dimensional geometry so that pupils can:

- describe, model, draw, and classify shapes;
- investigate and predict the results of combining, subdividing, and changing shapes;
- develop spatial sense;
- relate geometric ideas to number and measurement ideas;
- recognise and appreciate geometry in their world.

(NCTM, 1989, p. 48)

It is worth noting how well Eileen and Rena's approach met these different aims with the tessellations project.

Second, there is uncommonly good support available for this topic, both in the form of teacher workshops and printed materials (such as the book by Seymour and Britton, which was used by Eileen, Rena, and the children, and articles like the classic *How to Draw Tessellations of the Escher Type* by Joseph Teeters (1974)). Third, and perhaps most important, is the strong aesthetic appeal of the topic. Even if the geometric subtleties go unnoticed, the pupils almost invariably find the topic enjoyable and the results can always be rationalised as an exercise in visual art should the maths go flat in transit.

The immense popularity of the work of the Dutch artist Maurits Escher over the last twenty years (Ernst, 1985; Escher, 1974; Schattschneider and Walker, 1977) is a further indication of the aesthetic appeal of tessellating patterns. Unlike the eight-year-olds who generated such an impressive list of properties, however, very few purchasers of Escher posters are able to articulate even the most fundamental characteristics of tessellations, let alone speculate as to why they find these works so attractive.

Seen more generally, the topic of tessellations would seem to be a direct offshoot of a common and powerful human aesthetic urge, that of 'fitting'. The word 'fit', which occurs in English both as a noun and as a verb, is, at first glance, an innocuous term. It is, however, perhaps fitting (so to speak) to note that its connotations and connections are both numerous and rich. We speak of clothes that fit well and of a good fit between talent and task. The perennial appeal of jigsaw puzzles may well be linked to a general sense of satisfaction that comes from seeing pieces come snugly together to create a whole.

Snug fits are critical to the craftsperson; take, for instance, the observations made by Jim Locke, a carpenter profiled in Tracy Kidder's book *House* (1985):

> What quality means to me is how tightly things fit together. Joints are the essence of it to me. ... Usually, when you are done and there's a place where it's not quite perfect, you find a way to tighten it up.

The American writer John Jerome (1989), in *Stone Work: Reflections on Serious Play and Other Aspects of Country Life*, a book which deals with his construction of a long stone wall on his country property, makes much the same point:

Joinery, it now occurs to me, must be the foundation of all craft. You put two things together to make something else, to accomplish some purpose; the better they fit or work together, the greater the pleasure from the making.

(p. 31)

It may well be then that Rena and Eileen have, through this topic, touched on human instincts which transcend narrow academic boundaries. Human beings are pattern-seeking and pattern-creating creatures. Tessellations and tiling patterns have a long and culturally rich history. They can be seen as visual poetry. At a certain point, only one piece will do – no other will fit and the frustration of not having a piece of the 'right shape' is matched only by the satisfaction of seeing that the piece you need is the piece you have.

There is, I think, a feature of the current electronic entertainment world which supports some of this speculation, namely, the video game called *Tetris*. The pieces in *Tetris* are the seven distinct ways in which four (hence 'tetris') identical squares can be joined together edge to edge (the 'I' bar, the 'Tee', the two forms of 'L', the 2×2 square, and so on; see Figure 2.15).[5]

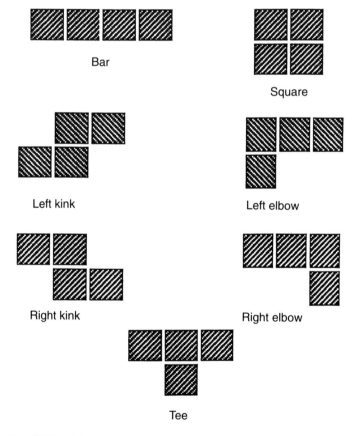

Bar

Square

Left kink

Left elbow

Right kink

Right elbow

Tee

Figure 2.15 Tetris tiles

The playing area is a 10 × 20 'well' into which the pieces are dropped at an ever-increasing pace. The player's task is to rotate and translate the pieces as they fall down the shaft of the well, so that a full, ten-unit line is created. When this happens the line disappears and the player has, for a moment or two, somewhat more room to manoeuvre. The most noteworthy feature of *Tetris* is that it has been immensely popular, both with males and with females, and to a lesser extent with adults as well as with children. The fact that this game has uniquely crossed gender and age barriers seems most likely to be a function of its strong appeal to the 'fitting' urge which is not something offered by other video games (Carlton, 1994).

Materials and the engagement of the intellect

Earlier in this chapter, both Eileen and Rena acknowledged the importance of aesthetic appeal as a factor in the choice of tessellations as a project topic. In particular, Rena felt that she could 'bluff through the mathematics of tessellations', based on her tongue-in-cheek observation: 'How complicated can a few polygons be?' In fact, knowing Rena, this question reflected her underlying confidence and willingness to explore some unknown paths, ones that she knew might not be simple ones. (It is perhaps of interest to mention that even though she was willing to explore a number of paths, she also genuinely backed off from pentagons.) For here, as is often the case, things which appear simple on the surface are, on closer examination, much more intricate and interesting than one may have initially assumed. Once realised, this awareness has very significant implications for educational activity.

In a society dominated by materialistic concerns, we too often underestimate the educational potential of the simple objects that surround us. (For an eloquent counter-example, see the work of the American philosopher and educator, David Hawkins (1964, 1974); and also Duckworth, Easley, Hawkins and Henriques (1990).) The deepest scientific and mathematical ideas do not emerge only from expensive kits, visits to exotic museums, computer simulations, or multimedia extravaganzas.

Einstein once noted that the most profound democracy is that of the intellect. The intellect operates at least as well on simple materials as on complex commercial technologies. The children's statements of logic and classification, such as 'all triangles tessellate', transcend the materials that generate these insights. These statements could come from either simple or complex materials. We need to ask whether materials are engaging the intellect in this way, and not whether the materials themselves are simple or complex.

Imagine the various ways these statements of logic and classification might have been generated. In this case, they were made on the basis of experience with ceramic tiles. What if the pupils had encountered tessellations in the context of a vivid and colourful set of tessellating images generated by a computer program such as *Tesselmania!*, a widely-used and enthusiastically-received computer environment created exclusively for exploring and creating tessellating patterns? Or what if they themselves programmed the colourful images on the computer screen, for instance using the Logo programming language?

In the case of the tiles, the contribution of a strong tactile component is obvious and central, an element that is missing from both computer scenarios. Tiles also offer a direct link to our day-to-day environments. However, constructing tessellations with tiles is time-consuming, and the creations are difficult to save, later manipulate, and/or share with others. With good teaching, these difficulties can be turned to advantage. As with all artistic endeavours where constraint is a fundamental feature, artistry comes from pushing against the limits of the constraints. In this case, for example, recognising the need to share or exchange creations once the tiles were returned to the tub, Rena helped the pupils see a need for creating notational systems.

The colour, speed, and power of computer feedback with computer environments like *Tesselmania!* are impressive and engaging, at least in the short term. However, with this power comes the danger of being mesmerised by the presentation rather than by the underlying ideas. I have observed children spending several hours with *Tesselmania!*, generating one tessellation after another, without showing any signs of analysing or attempting to understand the logic behind the images. On the other hand, this kind of analysis *can* occur when a teacher or a peer makes an observation or asks a question, moving the focus from image to issue.

From a different perspective, a computer programming language like Logo (Papert, 1980, 1985, 1993; Watt, 1983) offers the possibility of intellectual engagement in a broader way than *Tesselmania!*, but this kind of engagement is rare in practice. Since Logo became widely available in the early 1980s, many textbooks and curriculum guidelines have included Logo activities as suggested optional investigations. In the 1994 Ontario Provincial Standards for Mathematics, Grades 1–9, for example, Logo challenges are listed as standard assessment activities. Despite this suggested and, in some cases, mandated direction, relatively few classroom teachers have had the necessary support to be able to use Logo successfully. Why is this?

Fundamentally, teachers, in their own experience, have not had the power of Logo revealed to them to their own satisfaction, and so their use of it remains at a mechanical level. Also, Logo has neither the tactile appeal of tiles nor the speed nor the immediate visual appeal of *Tesselmania!* – an expectation children have of computer technology. It is not that speed and colour are impossible to achieve with Logo, but that these elements come only with considerable insight, extensive periods of application, and deep intellectual engagement.

The materials, therefore, do not guarantee that the intellect of children will be engaged. If the teacher does not recognise the possibilities in the materials, whether simple or complex, nothing significant is likely to follow. Materials are neither simply bad nor good, in and of themselves. The right combination of the potentiality of both ideas and materials provides the richest possible arena for the working of the intellect. In the ideal case, I would like to see tiles, *Tesselmania!*, and Logo *all* used for the study of tessellations, by a teacher who is fully aware of the strengths and limitations of each, who emphasises enquiry and construction of understanding through social interaction and directed discussion.

It follows that Eileen's use of construction paper should not be seen as pale in comparison with the use of ceramic tiles or computer technology. Likewise, the use of geoboards reached a new level of importance because of the way that the pupils had been engaged with these 'simple' ideas. As explorations with tessellations progressed, Rena moved away from the tiles to paper and pencil and grids. There is a fluid use of materials here. If Rena and Eileen had had a computer in the classroom, they would have invariably moved to that as well. I return to a discussion of the role of computers and information technology in a later chapter.

Amateurs, professionals, and simple ideas

Simple and complex materials in the classroom have a parallel in the arena of scientific and mathematical explorations with simple and complex ideas. What has been shown in a range of different scientific domains, much more clearly than was previously realised, is that complex phenomena are quite frequently the result of the repeated application of a small set of simple, interacting, factors. This insight has perhaps been most clearly demonstrated in the popular, colourful and active research area of non-linear dynamics, better known to the general public as the theories of fractals and chaos. (See, for example, the fine introductory book by James Gleick (1987) simply entitled *Chaos*.)

Cohen and Stewart (1995) deal with these ideas at length, coining the terms 'simplexity' and 'complicity' to describe two different types of interaction between simplicity and complexity. It may well be the case that major research problems, for example, the nature of certain diseases, can be understood by constructing a conceptual model based on a small number of rules. Hence, aided by the rapid power of computing tools, there has been considerable growth in fields like computational chemistry where scientists attempt to create new chemical compounds which may have desirable effects when used in a pharmaceutical role, by means of the simulated manipulation of molecular models.

An important related issue is the question of the public image of mathematics. To citizens whose exposure to the subject is likely to have been exclusively in the form of classical schoolroom practice – chalk and talk, texts and tests – the world of research mathematics in almost all cases seems completely alien. While not implying in the least that the vast majority of this work would be anything other than completely unfathomable to all but a few fellow experts, it is the case that many of the most creative of mathematicians can explain the origins and purposes of their investigations, if not their methods, to interested lay people. In some cases, it is still possible for an interested amateur to make a significant contribution to mathematical knowledge. The tessellation theme offers fascinating examples of both aspects of this phenomenon.

The starting point for my two examples is a long-standing question about the tessellating possibilities of pentagons. It is well known (at least in some mathematical circles – we will return to this in Chapter 6) that all triangles and all quadrilaterals tessellate. It is also the case that regular hexagons tessellate. For convex polygons with numbers of sides greater than six, it can be proven that no tessellating shapes exist. That leaves the question of polygons with five sides as an intriguing opportunity for investigation (perhaps one that Rena will return to the next time she explores tessellations).

It is relatively easy to demonstrate, either analytically (the angle sums just do not work) or empirically (if you build them they will not come together), that regular pentagons will not fill the plane. There are, however, many non-regular pentagons, usually defined in terms of their angle properties, which do tessellate. Being able to state with certainty, that is to say, to *prove*, that one has enumerated all possible different types of tessellating pentagon has proven to be a difficult challenge.

In 1975, the accumulated efforts of mathematicians (in particular, Kershner, 1968) over many decades were summarised by Martin Gardner (1975) in his widely-read column in *Scientific American*. (The German mathematician, David Hilbert, had made problems of this type one of his famous, 'mathematical challenges of the new century' lecture to the International Congress of Mathematicians in 1900.)

In San Diego, Marjorie Rice, a housewife and mother of five children, whose formal mathematical training had ended with a general course required for high school graduation at age 16, some 35 years before, picked up her son's copy of *Scientific American* and began to doodle. Over the next two years, this gifted amateur geometer (and here the etymological connections of the word 'amateur' to 'love' seem so appropriate) with some support from the geometer Doris Schattschneider (who has beautifully documented this story in a collection of essays dedicated to Martin Gardner) made discoveries which had eluded all of the learned scholars in the field.

In commenting on her elementary school education, Marjorie Rice noted:

'Arithmetic was easy and I liked to discover the reasons behind the methods we used. . . . I was interested in the colors, patterns and design of nature and dreamed of becoming an artist. . . .' Her later years at the school 'were enriched by two very fine teachers, Miss Keasey and Miss Timmons. ... When I was in the 6th or 7th grade our teacher pointed out to us one day the Golden Section in the proportions of a picture frame. This immediately caught my imagination and ... I never forgot it.'

(quoted in Schattschneider, 1981, p. 161)

It does not require a particularly powerful imagination to hear Rena and Eileen's children saying something quite similar should they come to reflect on their time in elementary school.

The second example comes from the work of a profound mathematical mind, that of Roger Penrose of Oxford University, but it begins with similar, simple materials, a sense of amateurish play and the same basic question of pentagonal tiling. Because of Penrose's mathematical ability, it ends with the creation of mathematical framework for the investigation of an exciting new scientific phenomenon, that of 'quasicrystals' (Edelson, 1992; Gardner, 1989; Penrose, 1989; Senechal, 1994).

British mathematician, David Singmaster (1988) situates Penrose's explorations in the following context:

My Polytechnic's coat of arms includes 'the net of half a dodecahedron', i.e. a pentagon surrounded by five other pentagons. In 1973 I wrote to Roger Penrose on a Polytechnic letterhead which shows the half dodeca-hedron. Penrose had long been interested in tiling the plane with pieces that could not tile the plane periodically and the letterhead inspired him to try to fill the plane with pentagons and other related shapes. He soon found such a tiling with six kinds of shape and then reduced it to two shapes which could tile the plane in uncountably many ways, but in no periodic ways. These have a generalised five-fold symmetry, and they are now called 'quasicrystals'.

(p. 363)

In a collection of interviews with contemporary cosmologists (Lightman and Brawer, 1990), Roger Penrose gave some insights into his mathematical interests as a child. Responding to a question about his early reading habits, Penrose stated:

Reading wasn't quite the thing I did. I never read much. ... I did do things like make models – polyhedra and so on. They were usually geometrical models, which I made out of cardboard. There were lots of things I made. I was very interested in doing things on my own.

Once again, the experience of this gifted scholar seems to resonate exceptionally well with the sorts of work done by Eileen and Rena with their mathematics pupils.

Chapter 3

Animation
'We're making a movie in maths'

RENA

Animation is not an undertaking for the faint of heart. Making an animated film, whether using traditional techniques or fancy technology, takes hours and hours of work. I hasten to add, however, that I grew tired of thinking about the several hundred drawings of trees and park benches that the children created for their film long before the children grew tired of drawing and painting all of those benches and trees. I am always amazed to see how long children's interest can be sustained in this kind of work when the result will be a film of less than a minute in duration. So much for the notion that eight-year-olds have short attention spans.

The children were keen on animation from the start. I mentioned animation as a possible project just before the Christmas holidays, and at the beginning of January the group was ready to roll. On my return after the Christmas break, Sam greeted me with: 'You know what I did all Christmas holidays? I thought about my animation. Do you think I could do an animation of an old man?'

Sam's opening remark led to a general discussion of films and animation, and so the animation project began.

Early explorations with moving images

When I asked the children about their ideas on animation and movies, it was clear they already knew animation was based on the notion of quickly showing a series of still images. As Doug put it:

> 'Well, it's like you draw pictures and make them fast like you sort of move them whatever you want to move, different shapes and stuff – say you wanted to make someone move, you could make him move slowly if you draw the pictures further away and if you want to make them move faster, like running, you move them [closer].'

They were sure, however, that 'big' movies were somehow different:

'That's acting.'

'It's not like animation.'

'Well, except like they use [animated] characters, like Aladdin ... or Muppets Christmas.'

'In real movies, they act.'

The children appeared to take on faith my claim that movies 'aren't real motion, [but] like animation, are a series of single photographs or slides played fast, fast, fast!' Someone responded with: 'So they take pictures of [actors]?' I answered yes, and then asked how many pictures they thought would make up one second of a movie. They guessed as low as 15 and as high as 300. Those who guessed as high as 300 justified their estimate by arguing that 'movies look so smooth, there have to be lots of pictures'. It turned out that the image rate that we would be using was 30 frames a second – a standard rate for video these days, I am told.

But why does a movie appear so smooth if it is truly a series of still images? At this point, we were ready to play with some images. Using thaumatropes (they are less familiar to children than flip books, but take far less time to make), it was relatively simple to convince them that an image is held in memory after it disappears from view, making the illusion of movement through a series of fast stills possible. A thaumatrope, as pictured in Figure 3.1, can be constructed from a piece of stiff card, so that the partial images on each side, when viewed together, form a complete picture.

In the example shown, the bird cage and bird combine so that the bird appears to be in the cage when the thaumatrope is 'engaged'. To engage the thaumatrope, two pieces of string are attached on either side of the card so that it can be twirled – and lo and behold, what we see is the complete image of a bird in a cage. Note that for the thaumatrope to work, the bird has to be upside-down in relation to the bird. This thaumatrope caused much wonder and amazement; as Hardeep pointed out with evident joy: 'Our eyes aren't quick enough. Technology is going faster than our bodies.'

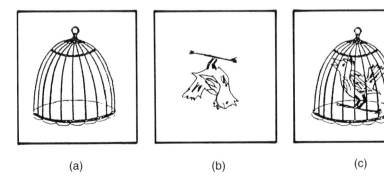

(a)   (b)   (c)

Figure 3.1 Thaumatrope of a bird in a cage

It is perhaps significant that Hardeep perceived this situation in terms of the power of technology, while Jennifer, seeing the head instead of the tail of the coin, said, 'That's neat! It's like your eye keeps a memory!', thereby attributing the 'cleverness' to humans rather than to the technology. This is in keeping with observations made by other researchers who have noted that girls tend to concentrate on human capabilities, while boys direct their attention to the technology (Inkpen *et al.*, 1994).

Several other issues came up in the thaumatrope investigations, including why one image had to be inverted in relation to the other, and why a right-side up image for the 'twirler' would be upside-down for the 'viewer'. A few theories were proposed – but I did not pursue this aspect of thaumatrope technology.

We spent about a half hour making our own thaumatropes. The children had some wonderful ideas – a turtle in a tank, a horse in a stable, a clock face on one side with hands on the other, a face with hair, nose and mouth on one side with eyes on the other, and a spaceship going through a wormhole. (This last was Hardeep's idea: he was passionate about the *Star Trek* series, and found ways to incorporate his passion and the knowledge that went with it into much of his work. See Chapter 4 on jewellery and Chapter 6 on children's ways of being mathematicians.) Jennifer made a face with eyes on the other side, and discovered, to her dismay, that she had miscalculated where the eyes should be placed. As a result, the creature's eyes appeared to pop in and out of his head. This 'mistake' made the rest of us howl with laughter and Jennifer began to laugh along, enjoying the attention and seeing the humour in her miscalculation.

My own thaumatrope was a pretty feeble effort – a triangle in a cloud. Jon was watching me draw the triangle and asked if I was trying a tessellation, cautioning me that a tessellation would be very difficult (and implying that I did not have a chance). I assured him that my idea was a much simpler one. The thaumatropes were a hit – the other pupils in the room clamoured around to see what the excitement was, and were assured that they would be involved in the animation project later in the process (we must have been pretty distracting to Eileen's group when we burst into laughter watching Jennifer's 'popping-eyes' thaumatrope).

At the end of the day, several of the children inquired about making thaumatropes at home. Erika piped up with: 'You can easily do this at home', and Tracey pressed for more details: 'Miss Upitis, can you do this on normal paper and not cardboard paper?' I was delighted by their interest – as I have mentioned before, if something is good enough (or real enough) to do in one's own time, then I am sure it is worth doing in the classroom as well.

While we were working on our thaumatropes, Andrea must have been thinking about the interaction of sound and still pictures, and from her questions was clearly puzzling over how one could create a movie out of still pictures with sound that would correspond quite accurately with the images.

It looks like actors are speaking the words, yet I had claimed that what was 'filmed' was a fast series of still pictures. Andrea pondered: 'When you said they keep on taking pictures, you don't get sound in pictures'.

I responded with a somewhat half-baked explanation of how the filming occurs at the same rate that the stills are shown, and that 'sound is recorded at the same time and laid on top, and that is just like an audiotape, like the one I am using now. When we do our animation, we will make the picture part, and then after, we will make a tape to put on top – the audio.' I am not sure if my explanation was enough for Andrea's inquisitive mind, but it was the best I could offer at the time. At any rate, the issue of sound did not come up again until months later, when we were ready to create the soundtrack for our animated film, when the sound/stills issue was revisited.

We tried a few other paper-based animation techniques before beginning to plan and create our film. The kinematoscope, a revolving wheel with four different images, was somewhat less successful than the thaumatrope, probably because the point had already been made and the children were ready to get on with the 'real' thing. We also spent some time transforming simple shapes, starting with a particular concave quadrilateral (the *Star Fleet Command* symbol, according to Hardeep), and trying flips, rotations, and scaling. I also had the children guide me in transforming a cat into a teapot, although that provided more entertainment than enlightenment as the children watched me draw, or more to the point, not draw. They also completed an exercise where the first and last frames were provided, and the task was to supply the missing frames. This was of great interest, since it had obvious application to cell animation where a good deal of drawing and transformation of the images would be involved.

Planning the film

Before entertaining ideas on the kind of story we might portray through an animated film, I showed the entire class a cell animation film that I had helped a group of ten- and eleven-year-olds produce a few years earlier. This animated sequence was presented as part of a school musical, and involved a series of singing barnyard animals. I told them that it was filmed at a rate of about 20 frames per second and that about 800 cells were created. We watched the film several times, and after the third showing, Jon volunteered that the film was '45.60 seconds long'. Despite the fact that I had a good sense of how much work would be involved, on seeing the barnyard scene again and watching the faces of the children, I was inspired to jump into another cell animation project.

And so we were off. The Grade 3 children came up with ideas faster than I could record them, and after about ten minutes of brainstorming, we began to group the ideas as the story started to emerge.

'We could do a barnyard.'
'With flying animals!'
'No, flying people.'

'We should have something that goes over time, like changes.'
'An old man.'
'Chopping down a tree.'
'Building a cabin!'
'No, a baby growing up and getting old and dying.'
'Growing a tree.'
'Or a tree in all the seasons.'
'Apples.'

'Space.'

'Someone drinking out of a glass.'

'And growing and losing hair.'

'It could have flowers blooming, like in the spring.'

'Someone could be knitting.'

'It should have changes.'

When the dust settled, it was relatively easy to pull out a story line. Consensus was quickly reached. The film would be about a person sitting on a park bench, ageing as the seasons passed, with several transformations over the seasons. These transformations would include changing trees, weather changes, growing flowers, apples falling from the trees and rotting, while, all along, the person aged: 'with his hair thinning out, body slumping', and finally: 'lying on the park bench [which, of course, had also changed over the seasons] and dying'.

There was a brief discussion about whether the person should be a man or a woman (Jennifer suggested a man made more sense since he was more likely to go bald), and whether he should die or go to sleep. (I was the one who suggested 'sleep'; the children insisted that he die, and the narrator could explain he was homeless.)

Most of the original features of the story remained over the three months that the film evolved, with only some of the detail (flowers and apples) abandoned early on. We had a short discussion about the length of the film, and taking 20 frames a second as the measure, decided that a 40-second film was about right.

We roughed out a sequence in 10-second intervals (how convenient that spring, summer, autumn, and winter divided so nicely into 40), and determined who would take charge of the various parts – tree, bench, man, background, and so on. Everyone chose something they felt attracted to and comfortable with, and all of the parts were spoken for in a few minutes time.

I joined Stephanie and Tracey on the 'background team' – I did not think my skills included drawing human figures. Tanya chose the tree, Andrea, the park bench, Erika and Jennifer, the man; as the project unfolded, it became clear that each of us had chosen something we could do well.

Producing the film

The children began by creating many rough sketches for each element of the film. These rough beginnings were quickly refined – Andrea's drawings of the park bench began to show perspective. Similarly, the tree began to look more realistic as Tanya started to pay closer attention to the trees in bud outside the classroom window (see Figure 3.2), and her sketches became more convincing as well.

We began to work in earnest. When it became apparent that an afternoon a week was not long enough to get our teeth into the project, I began coming in during some lunch hours, and children used some of their independent work time as well. Soon enough, I was coming in almost every lunch hour, over a period of several weeks. One day when I did not come, Andrea muttered with disappointment to Eileen: 'Miss Upitis isn't here? But we brought our lunch.' They carried on without me.

Our sessions began to take on the look of a production workshop. Sam and Jon happily cut cells from the recycled plastic report folders. Doug and Hardeep sprayed 'snow' with a toothbrush. Tracey and Stephanie and I worked on the background using a combination of water-colour pencil crayons, gouache paint, and a variety of brushes – my love of painting found its way into the maths classroom.

Tanya quietly worked away on her tree, occasionally looking up and reporting: 'I'm on tree two.' Often her short comments were pearls of understanding. When she was drawing her fourth or fifth tree, she noted if the tree stayed without buds for about a second, that would mean that the cell she was working on 'could be used for 20 frames'. As always, the children quickly picked up new vocabulary in the context of their work – words and phrases like 'cells', 'frames per second', 'templates', 'rate', 'growth', 'different proportions', and 'transformations' – animation words, but mathematical words as well.

Progress was slow and deliberate over the next weeks. It was the tree that took the most work – only in winter did it remain unchanged. Tanya steadfastly continued to work at her tree, making short reports every now and then ('I'm up to 45 buds and 5 cells'). All of the children made constant calculations while they were working, glancing at our original 800 frame/40 second chart, and quietly dividing and multiplying. Jennifer reported dreaming about 'the man' one night, and told me: 'It's all I've been thinking about.'

Figure 3.2 The evolution of a tree in bud

Unlike Tanya and Jennifer, some of the other children took on a variety of jobs rather than working on a single feature of the film. Sam and Jon not only prepared cells and paint for many of the sessions, but proceeded to make credits and titles for the film, using their home computers to create them. Jon then made the final version of the credits on his mother's computer at work, using the laser printer. (The dot matrix printer in the computer room at school was not good enough – *real* credits should be done on a laser!)

But where's the maths?

When I started the animation project, I knew there was a great deal of mathematics involved in producing an animated piece – not only computation, as in the counting of cells and calculating rates of change, but geometry and art in making transformations to objects over time. What was lovely was all of the unexpected mathematics that emerged. The examples I am about to describe happened over one lunch hour with eight children. At this point, we were already well into the project – many of the cells had been drawn and painted.

As I mentioned earlier, the tree required a great deal of drawing, since it changed from barren branches, to bud, to full leaves (which changed in colour), to autumn leaves, and finally, to barren branches once again. As Tanya worked on the tree, she began looking for help, and, on the day that these events occurred, she had formed a 'tree team' – not unlike part of a production team for a movie or for designing a piece of software. She had two other children drawing tree trunks and branches, reserving the drawing of the leaves for herself.

The difficulty they soon encountered was how to number the cells. Taking turns was not efficient, that is, it did not make sense for Stephanie to draw one, and then wait while Nicholas drew the next. Stephanie piped up with a solution: 'I'll do even numbers and you do odds'. Then Stephanie and Nicholas passed their drawings, in sequence, to Tanya for completion.

While the tree team was working away, Andrea was patiently drawing park benches. The park bench stayed in one spot for the entire film, but over the winter months (well, winter seconds) snow accumulated on the bench (an earlier idea to have the paint on the bench peel during the fall was abandoned part-way through the project). While drawing the fifth or sixth bench, Andrea had realised that she was simply drawing the same thing again and again, and said: 'I wish there was some way to photocopy cells'.

I realised that there was, kicking myself for not thinking of it sooner. A visitor to the classroom, who worked in an office with a photocopier capable of producing high-quality transparencies, offered to take a drawing of Andrea's and make multiple copies. At this point, others started to wonder if they too could take advantage of the photocopying of transparencies. Jennifer thought that she could have her man sit still while his hair colour changed, requesting 20 copies of the man in the 'fall [autumn] position'. And Tanya said: 'I could make a template of the tree trunk and we could use that for all the trees'.

At this point, the children began estimating how many cells of the same drawing they could use. Andrea thought that 50 would be enough for the bench to accumulate snow: 'since the bench is just changing in the winter, and that's about a quarter of them'. Thinking out loud, she then said: 'Maybe 60 would be better, in case we make mistakes painting. . . . no wait, 65.' Tanya made a similar calculation, and our visitor left with three drawings and requests for 20, 65 and 80 copies respectively.

While the tree, man, and bench groups were working as described (see Figure 3.3), Hardeep and Amber were painting the snow.

Figure 3.3 Tanya's trees

Here the idea was to introduce a thicker texture of white speckles with each subsequent cell, so that over time, it would look as if it were snowing more heavily. The first cell that Amber completed was a bit too dense, so I suggested that she make a cell 'before 1, and you can call it 0'. Hardeep quickly picked up that you could: 'move into negative numbers except negative numbers don't go on forever'. I told Hardeep that, indeed, negative numbers do go on forever, just like positive ones, and he replied: 'Oh. Well, after, say, negative 5, you would have no snow anyway. So it would be like going into another time zone or something.' Hardeep and Amber agreed that the snow would range from −5 to +5.

By this time, having determined the kind of video camera we were going to use to film *The Changes*, we had modified our frames/second ratio from 20:1 to 32:1. While the actual ratio was 30:1, I found it easier to think in multiples of four, and besides, 32 was a closer approximation to the actual rate than 20. Also, the camera we were using filmed at a fixed rate of four frames per 'click', so choosing 32 made sense. The children quickly caught on to working with the ratios, making statements like:

'So if it's 4 frames a click, then there's 8 clicks in a second, right?'

'It's a good thing we know our eight times tables.'

Meanwhile, Tanya was working on her own brand of estimation and calculation. She was working on the falling leaves sequence when the following interchange occurred:

Tanya: How many cells do I have 'til the end?
Rena: Sixteen.
Tanya: And there's sixty-one leaves. So how many should fall on each cell?
Rena: See if you can figure it out.
Tanya: We've only gone up to the 12 times tables.
Rena: Well, make an estimate, and I will multiply it out for you. [Tries 7, decides on 4.]
Tanya: The first tree already had seven fall, so should I make the next one eleven?
Rena: Yes. And then what?
Tanya: Well, fifteen, nineteen, . . . twenty-three.
Rena: That's it.

[After a few minutes]

Tanya: When leaves fall from the trees, they don't really fall at the same rate all the time. Maybe I should just leave a few for the end. And leave two or three to float.

Later, when Doug joined the tree team, Tanya gave him these directions:

Tanya: Thirty-four leaves for the next cell.
Doug: You mean draw thirty-four leaves?
Tanya: No, thirty-four leaves are *not there*. It's the other way around from the spring trees.

The final touches

When we were within days of filming (over two months after our initial explorations with thaumatropes), we accepted the help that the Grade 4 pupils kindly offered. Every child in the class had a chance to do some cell painting, and some of the Grade 4 pupils who had already helped over the lunch-hour sessions were happy to describe the process to their peers. It was during one of the full-class painting sessions that I overheard a conversation between Hardeep and Darren.

Hardeep: It took eight years to do the animation for *Beauty and the Beast*. Of course it's going to take us a while to do this one.
Darren: You mean they started *Beauty and the Beast* when I was only two years old?

It took us less than eight years to finish – in fact, we had our initial preview (with popcorn) some weeks before the soundtrack was completed. Adding sound was a relatively simple matter, especially since we had help from a former student of mine who had completed an undergraduate degree in film. Kerrie was a student teacher who had taken my Primary Mathematics Methods course the previous term at UBC, in Vancouver. When she heard about the animation project, she told me of her experiences as a film major and offered to help. She and I met to discuss soundtracks and one afternoon she came to the school to record some of the live sound effects – the man leaping for joy at the sight of spring, the rustling of autumn leaves, the winter storm, and so on.

I had the luxury of taking a back-seat role during Kerrie's visit, and watched with wonder as the children shared ideas, debated strategies, and recorded several variations of the sounds. The special effects were dubbed along with several other tracks (for more detail see Chapter 5), a narration provided by Andrea and Tanya, music improvised on the synthesiser and music recorded from compact discs. Together, these four sources of sound formed the final soundtrack. Since we had two channels or soundtracks to play with, the combined soundtrack was quite impressive – a fitting polishing touch to *The Changes*.

Not long after the animation film was completed, I happened to view a short documentary on animation while flying from Vancouver to Toronto. The documentary featured a number of new animation techniques and showed clips of people working in various animation studios. Some computer animation techniques were featured.

I was reminded of a conversation I had with Kori, a computer science graduate student, who had visited the classroom while we were deep in cell drawings. Kori had just completed a course in computer animation, and was interested in the children's animation efforts, noting their work involved the same kinds of decisions and tasks, although with less sophisticated technology, as the animation she herself had created earlier in the year. As she observed, animation is time-consuming no matter which tools are used.

One of the comments on the documentary on the flight was similar – the phrase used was 'demanding and often back-breaking'. Further, the commentator emphasised the importance of mathematics, stating that it was critical that the form and proportions of each character be united in the character's movements and relationship with other figures. One of the examples shown was an animated sequence using a doll that was capable of making many fine movements (and I found myself wondering if there was time to try just one more animation project before the year was out).

The documentary ended with a description of the joy that the artists and animators felt when they viewed their finished product. I wondered if any of the children in Eileen's class had felt enough joy that they too would become animators in another phase of their lives. Time will tell (at the rate of at least 30 frames per second).

EILEEN

When Rena first talked to me about doing an animation project, I knew her well enough to believe it would be possible, yet still not well enough to be unamazed. Like most teachers, I had taken classes on field trips to *Science World* and had played around with the moving picture machines there. I had even toyed with the idea of trying to make one myself, thinking it would be a great project. I recalled making a flip-book and remembered the amount of time, work, and co-ordination of effort that went into it. An animated film? Sure, go for it! As I found out, however, even for an observer and sideline participant, animation is indeed not a project for the faint of heart.

I could sense the excitement in the Grade 3 children right from the start. Rena brought in a thaumatrope and had her group making thaumatropes for themselves. These were fascinating devices that quickly demonstrated the adage that the hand is quicker than the eye. I was really impressed with this demonstration of retained imagery. My group of Grade 4s were interested in what was going on with the Grade 3s and they were allowed to test the thaumatropes for themselves with the understanding that they could develop some in their own time.

As noted earlier, this sharing of products had been a strength of our maths projects right from the beginning. Both groups knew they could participate, in some way, with the project of the other group. And, usually, each group made sure they knew what the other was doing on an ongoing basis. Some of the children tried to construct what they saw the other group doing and some were content just to be aware vicariously of the other group's progress.

What were the Grade 4s doing while the Grade 3s were learning the ins and outs of animation? They were beginning a study of symmetry. This study was going to take them from identification of plane, line, and rotational symmetry, to using symmetry and four-quadrant graphing for the creation of string art, to the design and construction of kaleidoscopes (see Chapter 5). I always tried to make my projects fit with Rena's in terms of both scope and mathematical concepts. There were many parallels between the two projects. Both involved a great deal of geometry, co-ordination and understanding of movement. Both resulted in moving pictures – the Grade 3s had a story line and the Grade 4s had lines of symmetry.

I also tried to select projects that would be of a non-interfering nature. My group was the larger of the two, and potentially the most boisterous, containing 12 boys and 4 girls. Ironically, it was during the animation project that I noticed times when the Grade 4s (and I) were disturbed by the activity of the Grade 3 group. Rena noted earlier that she was aware that the laughter of the Grade 3s might be a distraction to the other pupils (recall the eye-popping thaumatrope). On other occasions, she was not aware that the noise made by the Grade 3s was a problem. At these times, I asked myself whether the noise was distracting to my working group or just to me, and whether the disturbances caused by these short bursts were outweighed by the learning for both groups. One of the trade-offs of having informal learning situations is that concentration can be momentarily lost.

My role was to be involved actively with the Grade 4s and to create projects with them. At the same time, however, I decided that I could easily keep a finger in the animation project, and this is my chosen focus in this chapter. From this perspective – one from the sidelines – I will relate some of the sights and sounds of the Grade 3 animation project.

Animation is very animated. My memory of the whole project is itself something like a flip-book. I have a series of still cells, or scenes, in my mind's eye that, when viewed together in sequence, reproduce the project for me. Here are my frames.

Still number 1

Rena is at the flip-chart madly copying ideas that are being flung at her by the Grade 3 group. All of the pupils are enthusiastically involved in this process. I am struck by the sincerity of the contributors and by the positive way that everyone is entertaining each idea given. Even though I cannot really see or hear clearly from my vantage point across the room, I know that the topics being shared are reasonable and responsible by the way the group looks and sounds. My Grade 4 group is able to function effectively, without being distracted.

Still number 2

'We're going to be animators and we're going to make a movie.' This was no idle boast or whimsical dream. The Grade 3s fully believed they were capable of producing a movie. The attitudes necessary for success were in place. Trust, self-confidence, knowledge of resources, persistence, and willingness to learn were all evident. I sensed they would be able to sustain this commitment.

Still number 3

Another glance at the flip-chart. This time I see columns of numbers and hear lively discussion about 'how many frames would that take?' I see looks of concentration as the children mentally compute their suggestions. I am really impressed to see them using their newly acquired multiplication facts so gainfully and accurately. A real use for real knowledge.

Still number 4

I looked over at Tanya one day when she was working through her lunch hour on her trees and I was absolutely overwhelmed by the intensity of the involvement I was witnessing. Tanya fully believes that she will be an artist when she is older and also has a goal of self-sufficiency. She wants to live in a home she has built by herself, surrounded by gardens that she tends. After watching her painstaking process with the drawing and planning of trees, I fully believe Tanya will be, and will do, anything she desires.

Being able to stand aside and watch this project gave me a wealth of informal assessment data on some of my pupils that would not have been available to me in any other way. For example, observing Tanya's development as an artist from a spectator's role was quite different from watching as her teacher. I more easily saw the whole child and her deep involvement. As her teacher, usually I would be looking for more specific observations – how was she blending colours? How was she creating her impressions? Was she working well with others?

In moving away from standardised measures of development towards more descriptive and wholistic ways of reporting children's progress, teachers are constantly observing children with the intent of 'gathering authentic data'. The children in our classes are better watched now than ever before. Part of me feels a little uncomfortable with this. And it was this part of me that benefited from 'letting go'. Rena was the teacher in charge; I could relax my observation style. I learned how to watch the whole scene again, the 'big picture', and for this I am thankful. I think that prior to this project I must have often missed the forest for the trees.

At this point, I was becoming aware that the roles Rena and I had originally assumed, like the film, were evolving. Our responsibilities were growing less distinct; as Rena became more of a teacher, I found myself becoming more of a researcher.

In these evolving roles, the pupils saw and heard how Rena and I planned and informed each other of our progress. Our deliberate and overt real-world collaboration was readily picked up by the pupils, in that I began to notice a more collaborative tone to group work. Listening to each other became as valued as talking; learning to listen can be difficult for children (and adults alike).

Still number 5

During another lunch hour, I watched a handful of my Grade 4s hovering around the doorway to the class, wondering if they were intruding, yet wanting to be invited to join the activity. I, too, wondered what their status would be on this voluntary part of the project. So, I waited. When the Grade 3s were all busy, Rena quietly let the Grade 4s edge closer and slowly assimilated them into the group. The Grade 4s did not need to ask many questions on this day, and those questions that they did ask were directed to the Grade 3s. The Grade 3s carefully explained what was going on and the Grade 4s quietly assumed a helping role. The Grade 4s were quite willing to take their instruction from the Grade 3s who were, once again, the experts. The atmosphere of these voluntary noon-hour sessions was intense, quiet, and self-directed. I could feel there was something special in the air.

Still number 6

There was one afternoon session when Rena and the Grade 3s needed additional help to paint the cells. All the planning and outlining of images was completed, only the repetitive tasks of painting and filling-in remained. The class was split into three work stations based on their natural, in-class seating arrangement which was shaped like a giant U. Each group was a blend of Grades 3 and 4, boys and girls. All groups had three assignments to complete: one where they worked with me on a maths problem, one where they wrote an entry in their journals followed by independent reading, and one where they worked with Rena on the animation project.

The children remained stationary and Rena and I moved our things at 45-minute intervals. Rena, with the help of the Grade 3s at each table, gave some brief instructions and a short demonstration of the work that needed to be done. Each group completed more than we had originally estimated, with no flare-up of tempers or spilling of paint. Co-operation and a sense of purpose were the order of the day.

Still number 7

During the project, Rena occasionally had visitors in the room. Some of these were students of hers from the university, others were acquaintances and colleagues from other parts of her life. Some visitors came for the noon-hour sessions, some joined us for our maths projects period. All of the visitors had prior experience with animation. The pupils soon realised these were no mere observers, and before long, the children would have the visitors deeply involved in the work that was being done that period. I marvelled at the self-confidence of these Grade 3s. They responded to the expertise that was offered as easily as if they were reading a well-loved book. (After all, a resource is a resource.) The pupils knew the language of animation and could converse at a fairly skilled level, even with experts.

Still number 8

Rena announced the film was ready for viewing. Everyone was excited. The mood was created – the aroma and crunching of fresh popcorn filled the air. Ready, set, play.

'Was that it? Is it over?'

Our audience was not used to 40-second videos. We played it again, and this time Rena gave them a few prompts of what to watch for.

'Look to see how the seasons change.'

'Watch how the man changes – see if you notice any other changes.'

We watched it again. This time the class reacted with spontaneous applause. It took about three more viewings before the class was ready to discuss the product and very astutely agree that the title, *The Changes*, was a good one.

Still number 9

Soundtracks are complex, noisy undertakings. The practice stage of the soundtrack was one of the few times when the Grade 4s were really disturbed by our dual-track projects, as opposed to the times when the noise did not distract in a significant way, as noted earlier. This distraction did not last long, because Rena soon found space outside the classroom that prevented our being disturbed and allowed for absolute quiet when her group was ready to record.

However, as soon as she and her group had gone, I felt disappointed. I realised, then, how much I felt a part of this project even though I was always on the periphery. I also realised how much I was having to learn from the sidelines and I felt a little cheated. I wanted to see how sound-tracking happened. So, I went in search of the recording site – tracked them down, so to speak. I found them in time to hear the 'whoop' when the man on the bench jumped for joy at the arrival of spring. The group had to decide how long the whoop needed to be in order to last the number of frames that this action took, and then they had to co-ordinate their voices. More mathematics.

If I have one regret, it is that this part of the animation project took place outside of the classroom. The Grade 4s could have learned as I did, from the sidelines, about making a soundtrack. They could have worked through the noise and we could have stopped our work to ensure silence for the recording time. (The value of hindsight and reflection is powerful.) True, the Grade 4s would not *really* know what making a soundtrack was like, or how to make their own, but they would have gained some vicarious knowledge of the process. They would have had a mental set established for doing such a project should the opportunity present itself in the future.

The value of observing each other's work was made even more apparent to me at the end of the school year. When I asked the children to reflect back on maths projects, several of the Grade 3 children said that one of their favourite projects was the line drawings, and produced line drawings as illustrations for their journal entry. Interestingly, line drawings was a project undertaken only with the Grade 4s (see Chapter 5). Conversely, several of the Grade 4 pupils claimed that animation was their favourite maths project, and animation was primarily a project for the Grade 3 pupils. A number of the pupils felt involved in all of the projects Rena and I had developed, regardless of whether the projects were undertaken by the Grade 3s, the Grade 4s, or both.

Closing musings about animation

At this time, I do not think I will attempt an animation project in a traditional classroom setting on my own. By this, I mean a self-contained room, with one adult and thirty children. Why? Because it requires too much guidance, overseeing, and careful mediation. It also requires a high level of energy, expertise, and co-ordination. Pupils and teacher need patience, persistence, and the opportunity to work for long stretches without interruption.

However, I hope to try animation as a small-group project. After seeing how a group of ten can create a movie successfully, I am confident that I, too, could orchestrate a film of similar scope. How will I be able to engineer working with a group of ten? Well, I might use parent volunteers to work with the other pupils, or I might try it when I have a student teacher in the classroom. I could even sponsor a club, organised to meet out of school hours.

Perhaps after experiencing the process with a small group, I would feel prepared to try it with a whole class. Of course, I would still use parents, student teachers, and pupils who had already participated in animation, as helpers.

As Rena said at the beginning of this chapter: 'Animation is not an undertaking for the faint of heart.' However, because of the mathematical power that it creates in pupils, I feel it is a project well worth the considerable effort and time commitment that it entails.

BILL

The work of the children on the animation project described by Rena and Eileen raises, once again, a rich and extensive list of educational and mathematical issues. Before commenting on some of these, I think it important to note my thoughts on seeing the completed video. I had been well prepared for this, having had several conversations about the project, as well as having read a number of draft versions of Rena's and Eileen's sections of this chapter.

Despite this, my immediate reaction to the first few seconds of *The Changes* was that I had made some mistake – surely this could not be the work of eight- and nine-year-olds. And yet, it was. By the time that I had seen the first four or five seconds (120–150 frames), there were enough clues, both in terms of content (the story line suited perfectly) and level of sophistication (a slight jerkiness in places), for me to know that I had indeed inserted the right tape.

The video was everything that had been promised: poignant, profound (a sense of 'out of the images of babes'), and in its own unique way, quite charming. The balance between music and motion was artfully done, and its soft, washed colours and minimalist representations made it seem almost Japanese in its overall aesthetic impact.

Even after having watched it many times through, the strongest memory (akin to Eileen's stills) of the animation for me is that briefest of periods at the beginning of my first viewing, when – like miscounting the number of steps on descending a familiar staircase – I had the pit-of-stomach-fluttering experience of 'this is not what I had expected – something is out of place here – this is too polished to have been produced by children'. But it had been. So had the previous artifact which had prompted this feeling, for I had had a similar reaction on opening up my painted silk tessellation Christmas card.

These are observations which beg large questions.

(a) Is it really true that these artifacts are
    (i) of such high quality, and
    (ii) of such significance to children?
(b) Is it the case that this sort of experience is both
    (i) very desirable from an educational perspective, and
    (ii) extremely rare in most educational practice?

From my vantage point the answers are: (a) (i) yes, (ii) yes; and (b) (i) yes, (ii) yes. Questions for part two, now become: Why should this be? What are the significant factors at work here? Is it: (a) the *children*, (b) the *teachers*, (c) the *content* being taught, or (d) the *method* by which the content is being approached? Even mildly experienced multiple-choice veterans will want to add another choice here, namely '(e) all of the above', and in some senses that must be seen as the only possible right answer. Clearly, it would be impossible to separate any one of these factors completely from the other three.

Nevertheless, I want to argue that the ranking of the contributing factors, from the most significant to the least significant, is: (1) teachers, (2) method, (3) content, and (4) children. This is by no means to minimise the abilities of these young people: they are clearly an engaging and able group and, not insignificantly, there is a civilised number of them. The point is that there are, I am convinced, many groups of children like these in schools (and out of schools too, for that matter) all around the world.

It is perhaps worth noting here that I have observed Rena unleash similar sorts of magic on much less prepossessing groups of children. The school that generated the earlier 'model' animation for this exercise, for example, is one that would make many an experienced pedagogue ponder an immediate future in plumbing or real estate.

Nor is it the case that the content area can be lightly dismissed. The combination of art, music, technology, and mathematics lends itself to the exercise of the human imagination in ways that few other areas could surpass. And yet, it is quite easy to imagine Rena and Eileen getting similar sorts of responses from children while working in areas like language, history, or other sciences – indeed, by the end of this chapter, I will show how some of those sorts of connections could have been made with the animation project itself.

The key elements at work here are, in my view, the closely intertwined factors of who the teachers were, and the ways in which they chose to work with the children. First, and perhaps most important, are Rena's and Eileen's knowledge of, and attitudes toward, the content or curriculum they are bringing to the children. They know a lot about the topics in question and they are clearly eager to know more. They enjoy playing with these ideas, pushing the limits of their own knowledge and demonstrating the satisfactions that come from this sort of activity. In short, they know, they care (both about the curriculum and the children), and they want to share.

The second important point is the way in which they choose to share these ideas. The traditional school structure puts a premium on 'teacher telling' activities. In mathematics classes, the typical 'telling' teacher does not base his or her remarks on a passion (at least not a positive one) for the discipline. Often, the best one can hope for in such settings, as a pupil or a parent, is a reasonably firmly held belief that maths is useful.

While not untrue, this perspective is a far weaker basis for working with children than the one brought to bear by Eileen and Rena. The view which they exemplify is that mathematics is a fascinating and important human construction; a component of a broad range of activities which offer much satisfaction. Unlike the stereotypical classroom which is teacher-, textbook-, and technique-dominated, Eileen and Rena's approach is exploratory, open-ended, product-driven, and community-oriented.

Choosing content

Having made the argument that content is less important than the teachers and the method, the choice of content is nevertheless a significant one. The theme of change which Rena and Eileen chose to work with here is an exceptionally profound one. It is also, as this episode clearly shows, of great interest to children, and it is one to which they bring a number of very creative ideas. How many of them, one wonders, have kitchen or closet door frames at home where ever-increasing patterns of marks note their annual measurement of height?

We have seen glimpses of the visual, mathematical, and musical potential of this topic for young learners. It is also a central issue for much older learners in fields like history, biology, and management studies. The seeds for significant continuing research questions in fields like psychology and computer science are clearly observable here. For example, the question of the number of frames per second necessary for humans to interpret a process as being continuous is one which has interested film-makers from the earliest days. The term 'flicks', used to refer to motion pictures, dates back to the early days of film making when the 'flickering' frame rate of 18 per second was not sufficiently rapid to make humans perceive a fluid movement.

This question, in a range of related forms, highlights a central issue of the so-called digital age. In computer graphics, it appears in the area of 'screen resolution'; more expensive monitors have smoother, less-jagged pictures. In the area of digitised sound, the question becomes that of choosing an appropriate sampling rate, so that the auditory effect of a sequence of discrete bits is, for most purposes, indistinguishable from the original continuous 'wave' of sound.

The mathematical questions generated by these digital-to-analog-and-back-again applications (this characterises the nature of computer modems, for example) are challenging and central to progress in telecommunications. Error-correcting codes developed by research mathematicians over the last three decades are a key component in the development of technologies for data storage (as with compact discs) and security.

Many years ago, psychologist Jerome Bruner (1966) suggested that any concept could be discussed with children of any age in some suitable form. Bruner's conjecture was greeted by much scepticism on the part of most psychologists and educators, but the observations made by many of the children as they worked on and reacted to the animation project support the essence of Bruner's claim in a fundamental way.

For what we see here, among other things, is an advanced sensitivity to the concept of change and related ideas like cycles and rhythm. The children are using computation (arithmetic) at a level well beyond the standard curriculum for Grade 3 pupils. Both the accounts of experienced teachers and the standard research literature would tell us, in fact, that twelve-year-olds might well have problems with many of these calculations, yet these eight-year-olds were handling them comfortably. Why should this be so?

In keeping with previous remarks, the fact that this experience is authentic for both the children and their teachers is critical. Going back to Bruner's claim that children of any age can work with all manner of concepts, in a related stream of more recent research, scholars like Jean Lave (1988, 1991) have shown the remarkable abilities of learners in contexts of 'situated cognition'. Within this frame, it is common for what are usually perceived as difficult computations to be carried out without the usual frustrations.

Nearly two decades ago, Margaret Donaldson (1978), in her book *Children's Minds*, also revealed the importance of situating computations in settings that have meaning for children. This work of Bruner, Donaldson, and Lave spans three decades. It would not be difficult to find thinkers like them going back to the earliest part of the century. And yet, these are voices which have not generally been heard in mathematics education circles. Perhaps by combining the voices of these scholars with the voices of the children in classrooms like Rena and Eileen's, the resulting chorus would find an audience.

What makes the animation project an example of 'situated cognition', to use Lave's term? It is not coincidental that the topic is from an area close to 'where they live', that of animation. To a generation raised on Saturday morning cartoons and the prominence of Aladdins, Beasts, Beauties, Pocahontases, Simpsons, and Lion Kings, animated video has a reality that few older adults can imagine. It is very largely in this sensitivity to the reality of children's lives, and perhaps most importantly, to their imaginations, that much of the gift of teachers like Eileen and Rena resides.

Consider the long-term effect an experience like this might have on these fortunate pre-adolescents. Some eight or nine years later, in a context that is, almost definitely, and probably unfortunately, very different from that of the animation workshop, some of these young people and their peers may well be 'introduced' to the early ideas of subjects like trigonometry and calculus.

The history of most learners' experience with these subjects has been one of difficulty and frustration. When attempting to understand why this might be so, a central theme seems to be a 'lack of connection'. Where do these ideas, about rates of change, velocity, rotations, cycles, and continuity come from? Why should anyone (especially me) care? Such are the musings of many a young adult, but not, if all has gone well, with these fortunate early animators. For in this animation project, they have begun to grapple with a particularly fertile situation: one of a large number of 'real-world' situations where these ideas are fundamental.

Extending content

One characteristic of powerful choices for situated content is that they manifest themselves in a broad range of areas of human interest. This claim can easily be made for the change theme. The obvious ones – such as how do buds grow on real trees? – are perhaps already clear to teachers who have an eye for integration. I now provide some variations on this theme which may be less well-known, beginning with one from the area of language.

A language game, variously known as 'doublets', 'word links', or 'word ladders', begins with two words which have the same number of letters. The challenge is to try to create a chain of links from one word to the other. For a move to be legal, exactly one letter is to be changed, and the new configuration of letters thus formed must also be a recognisable word. Beginning from the word 'path', for example, legal first moves would include those to 'pith', 'pats', 'bath', 'hath', and (in North America) 'math'. Depending on the two words in question, there may be a number of solutions, only one solution, or no solutions at all. There are, for example, at least two different ways to change 'CAT' to 'DOG'. Somewhat more demanding classic challenges are to change APE to MAN, ONE to TWO, HEAD to TAIL, and WINTER to SUMMER.

It should not be hard to see that what we have here is a linguistic version of animation – perhaps we could now think of it as 'language morphing' – moving a step at a time from one state to another, with each state differing in only a minor way from its neighbours, with each being a distinct way-station on a well-connected path. The immediate connections to structural features of (the English) language are clear – routes from words beginning with the letter 'q', have, for instance, obvious limitations. Nor is it surprising that a master wordsmith like author Vladimir Nabokov (1962) would incorporate a version of the game into his novel *Pale Fire* under the name of 'word golf'. What might be more surprising is how scholars in other fields have found structural parallels in this activity. The distinguished biologist John Maynard Smith (1964), for instance, has noted parallels between 'doublets' and 'the limitations of molecular evolution':

> I suggest that a population of organisms which cannot now produce a particular protein X cannot evolve the capacity to do so unless X is connected by a series of unit steps ... to a protein it can now make.
>
> (p. 253)

The contemporary mathematician and science fiction author, Rudy Rucker (1982, 1987, 1994), sees similarities (Gardner, 1994) between doublets and formal mathematical systems in that in both cases one starts from an 'axiom' and by following a set of 'transformation rules' arrives at a 'theorem'. The path from initial state, or axiom, to theorem is, in this sense, a mathematical proof. As in mathematics, special pleasure is taken in knowing that one has found the shortest of all possible routes. This mathematical interpretation is perhaps not surprising in light of the history of this activity, for it was given to the world by one of the best known of all writer-mathematicians, Lewis Carroll, the author of *Alice in Wonderland*. Carroll (1879) first proposed the term 'doublets' in an article in the magazine *Vanity Fair*. His inspiration came from the 'witches' lines in *Macbeth*: 'double double, toil and trouble', and doublets quickly became a very popular Victorian pastime.

More recently the highly-respected Stanford University computer scientist, Donald Knuth (1978), winner of the computer science equivalent of the Nobel prize, has redirected his formidable talents to a computer-based analysis of aspects of doublets (Gardner, 1994). Starting from a list of 5,757 of the most common five-letter words in English (he found this to be the most interesting length of word), Knuth constructed a graph by joining each word with a line to those words which differed from it in only one place. This necessitated the drawing of some 14,135 lines. Knuth's analysis revealed the existence of some 671 words [such as earth, ocean, laugh, first, third, and ninth] which have no neighbours, and 103 word pairs which have no neighbours except each other, like 'odium-opium'. The two words with the highest number of connections were 'bares' and 'cores', each having 25.

As a final example of some of the structural richness of 'doublets', I take an example from the prolific mathematical expositor Ian Stewart (1995), in his recent book *Nature's Numbers: The Unreal Reality of Mathematical Imagination*. This text is one of a series entitled *Science Masters*. These books attempt to explain different branches of contemporary science to the so-called intelligent lay person. In any such endeavour of popularisation, a mathematician must tackle the difficult problem of how to exemplify one of the most critical distinguishing features of mathematics, that of proof.

In this context, it is interesting to note that Stewart approaches this subtle problem from the perspective of 'doublets'. Having explained the rules of the enterprise, he takes as an example the two terms SHIP and DOCK and gives as an example of a solution the chain: SHIP, SLIP, SLOP, SLOT, SOOT, LOOT, LOOK, LOCK, DOCK. Observing that other, and sometimes shorter, chains exist, he suggests that all chains which are solutions to this problem will have one feature in common, namely that at least one of the intermediate words will contain two vowels. He then leads the reader through a logical argument which shows that this must, in fact, always be the case: that is to say, he offers a proof of the 'SHIP/DOCK' theorem.

Closing thoughts on the issue of 'integration'

These examples from the domains of language, biology, computer science and mathematics share, with the animation theme, a common starting point – namely that of change. This kind of integration, where exploration of an idea moves fluidly from one area to another contrasts greatly with what passes for integration in many elementary classrooms. A list of sums on orange pumpkin-shaped paper in late October is neither good mathematics nor good art. To call it integration is to compound the fraudulence of the exercise. (For a similar view on this issue, see Jardine, 1995.)

Having written this section of the chapter, I very much wish that I could have had the opportunity to bring these ideas to Eileen's classroom, and to develop them with Rena and Eileen and the children. Perhaps if we had explored the connections to language, for example, Eileen would have developed ways of including animation as a 'regular' class activity. My sense of what would have happened with the injection of these ideas, had time and space not restricted us, is that we would all have been stimulated and excited, as the children were with the work that they had done in producing the animated film. As well, we would have emerged with a broader under-standing of the rich potential of the theme of change and a deeper understanding of mathematics and its connections to other intellectual domains.

Chapter 4

Paper jewels

'If you use isosceles, you get a bump in the middle'

RENA

When I was in Grade 5, and bored in class one day, I took a small triangular piece of paper and wrapped it around my pencil. I removed the paper from the pencil, tightened the roll I had started, and shot the paper missile across the room. I was not the only child amusing myself in this way, but, unfortunately for me, I was the only one who got caught. When asked what I was doing, with an incriminating piece of paper rolled on my pencil, I answered: 'Making something'. Somewhere along the line, I had learned that this expression would get me out of all kinds of trouble – my father's basement workshop had many fascinating tools and substances in it, and I had been caught messing around, and escaped punishment in this way before (except at home, I always said: 'I'm making something for *school*').

My Grade 5 teacher, no doubt disbelieving, answered, 'Making what?' And for some reason, I answered, 'A necklace'. And in this way, for me, the idea of making paper jewellery was born. For over twenty-five years, I have been making paper jewellery. For the last ten, I have made such jewellery with children. Despite the countless experiences I have had watching children twist and roll paper, I am always amazed at the lovely things they create from paper scraps, and I marvel at the emergence of new designs, year after year.

Playing with paper – the maths

Using paper as a medium for jewellery is attractive for many reasons. Paper is easily manipulated by young children, it comes in endless varieties of colours, patterns, and textures, and it is inexpensive – a fistful of paper from the recycling bin is good for several pairs of earrings and a necklace, at least. For this project, we used magazine paper, construction paper, sandpaper, cardboard, wrapping-paper samples (left over from a fund-raising sale from years past – Eileen saves everything), wallpaper samples, tissue paper, and regular bond paper.

Although we did not make use of home-made (or school-made) paper,

paper-making and paper jewellery could be combined. Many teachers and their pupils have made paper in their classrooms, recycling construction paper, newsprint, and so on, to create writing paper or paper sculptures. Using this kind of paper, in addition to the ones listed above, would not only enrich the choices for paper jewels, but extend the familiar activity of paper-making to a new context.

The instructions we gave to the children were relatively simple. We invited them to cut various shapes from the paper, and then to roll the paper or in some other way turn it into a three-dimensional object from the flat two-dimensional piece of paper. I am particularly fond of the effect that comes from rolling a long right-angled triangle, and I demonstrated this effect to the class. I took a full piece of magazine paper and cut a thin right-angled triangle, with a base of about $1\frac{1}{2}$", tapering to a point, and then rolled it tightly, gluing the tip in place with a glue stick. The result was a cylindrical tube with one end fatter than the other. I use these tubes for both necklaces and earrings (see Figure 4.1).

Many children experimented with triangles of different kinds, varying the type of triangle (e.g. scalene, isosceles, right-angled) and the size (experimenting with different bases and heights). Some rolled many pieces of paper before deciding on the shape they liked best – others took what they got from their first attempt and continued to build from there.

Tanya was one of the children who rolled many pieces of various shapes before deciding on the form she would finally pursue. She began by making a cylinder from the right-angled triangle as I had demonstrated, and then systematically tried different kinds of triangles. I heard her mumble: 'If you use isosceles, you get a bump in the middle' as she dropped her isosceles-triangle cylinder back in the paper bin. After about 20 minutes of folding and bending, Tanya had nothing more to show for her efforts than a pile of paper scraps. But another half-hour later, Tanya had crafted a delightful pair of earrings, both incorporating and rejecting what she had discovered through her explorations.

Tanya decided to use two triangles of different lengths to make the bodies for her earrings. I had also spoken about symmetry, and about how the centre of a person's face is the line of symmetry, so that to make the earrings look 'right' (that is, conventionally speaking), they would have to be mirror images of each other. Often children will make two identical earrings, and after putting them on, exclaim that they 'look funny'. When Tanya came to show me her two earring bodies, the following interchange occurred between us:

Rena: Oh! One is longer than the other. Did you know that?
Tanya: I don't want them to be the same and I don't want them to be symmetrical. They don't both have to be the same, do they?
Rena: No, you can make them any way you like. I just wanted to be sure that you knew they were different.

Tanya: Yeah, I know. And the shorter one is fatter too. So they kinda go
            together.

Not only did Tanya know that her two earrings would be of different
lengths, but she had also considered how to balance those lengths, by making
the shorter one with a larger diameter. I was reminded of a comment made
by one of my music theory students, studying harmony, who said that he
wanted to know the rules of harmony so he would know which rules he was

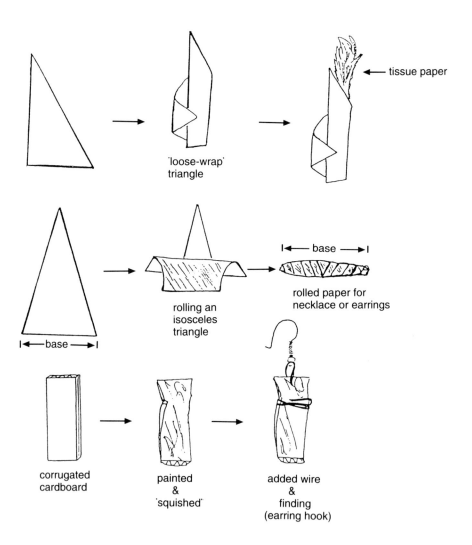

Figure 4.1 Methods for making paper jewellery

breaking when writing his own compositions. Tanya understood symmetry and equal lengths well enough to reject them both.

Once the bodies for earrings or a brooch or necklace have been made, there are a few more steps before the jewellery is complete. Many children choose to decorate the paper pieces, either by adding beads or by painting directly onto the paper surface. I usually provide a variety of inexpensive and varied beads, and let the children sort through them, looking for pairs of similar beads or, as in Tanya's case, looking for beads that somehow complement one another but are not necessarily the same.

When I first watched children sorting beads, I remembered using attribute blocks for sorting along the dimensions of shape, size, and colour. The children were doing the same kind of sorting here – but the sorting was purposeful; in order to make the kind of jewellery you have in mind, you sometimes have to sort along a number of different dimensions or attributes before the right beads are found. Sorting is an activity that is often limited to the early primary grades, but there is much to be learned by sorting and classifying as more complex sets of objects are introduced.

Some people never stop sorting and classifying – after all, biologists spend their lifetimes sorting and describing independent and overlapping sets of objects. Donald Knuth, a prominent computer scientist mentioned in the last chapter, speculates there are enough new problems in biology alone to keep scholars occupied for the next 500 years. (Bill discusses Knuth's work extensively at the end of the next chapter.)

Once children have made the bodies of their jewellery out of paper, and chosen beads if they so desire, they need to find a way to attach all of the pieces together. Wire works well. I provided the class with a variety of wire – telephone wire (left over from rewiring one of the buildings at the university for new computers, and destined for a land-fill site until someone thought I might be able to use it), copper electrical wire, and even a bit of jewellery wire in gold and silver colours.

I tend to avoid using commercial products explicitly designed for jewellery-making for two reasons: they are expensive, and often less interesting than the recycled materials that can be used. The telephone wire, for example, is a fine alternative to jewellery wire – not only does it find another life in someone's earrings or brooch, but the colours are great – blue and white stripes, yellow, green, orange, mauve – in fact, telephone wire comes in just about every colour imaginable. Another advantage to using it is that it is soft – strong enough for jewellery, but easy to bend by hand and cut with scissors, eliminating the need for pliers or wire cutters.

I might also add that using found materials, like magazine paper and telephone wire, is a genuine way to reuse these items. Not only do the materials get reused, but they do not end up in the garbage bin again a week later – these paper jewels are often worn for many years. I still wear a pair that I made fifteen years ago – not bad for eight cent earrings. While I have seen many projects requiring the use of recycled newspapers, toilet paper rolls, egg cartons, and the like, I have also seen many of these projects displayed for a week or two before making their way back to the bin. I try to keep an eye on the ultimate fate of creations from materials of any kind, and make choices accordingly. These are issues Eileen and I discussed with the children as well, and we found them to be highly sensitised to recycling the first time, but less aware of the ultimate fate of the materials.

But I digress: back to our environmentally-friendly paper jewels. Once the children have wrapped their wire around the bodies of their creations, adding beads, and attaching the 'findings' (the earring hooks or pin clasps), we move to a less environmentally-friendly step. (This is not a perfect world.) We provided the children with liquid plastic for dipping their creations. There are water-based plastics that can be used, but I have yet to find a water-based product that works as well as the liquid plastic used for finishing floors.

Because the jewellery is small in scale, very little of the plastic liquid is required, and with windows open, the fumes are tolerable. The liquid plastic not only gives the jewellery a brilliantly shiny finish, but also serves to fix the paper and beads in place permanently. If the glue stick does not hold the paper in place, liquid plastic certainly will. Once the jewels are dipped, they are hung on a line to dry. We rigged up a drying rack in the cloakroom, running strings between chair backs along the length of the cloakroom, placing newspapers underneath to catch any stray drips.

Playing with paper – another curriculum

We included paper jewellery as a maths project because of the many aspects of mathematics involved in making objects from paper – visualising the spatial transition from two to three dimensions, estimating and measuring sizes and materials, learning more about triangles and other polygons, and encountering symmetry, design, sorting, classifying, and counting in the process of creation. But we also had social reasons for introducing paper jewellery. Perhaps more than any of the other projects, paper jewellery lent itself best to dealing squarely with issues of gender and mathematics.

There is no question that making paper jewellery, at first blush, sounds like an activity that would appeal primarily to girls (even though most of the famous jewellers I can think of are men). When I introduced the idea to Eileen's class, I could see a few of the boys were uncomfortable with the idea, snickering to each other or turning up their noses. I was uncomfortable about this; I do not like children to distance themselves from an idea simply on the basis of gender connotations. And I was uncomfortable even though I knew that once everyone got involved in the project, they would probably enjoy it, learn a lot and want to do it again.

My discomfort made me wonder about the number of times I did *not* have a similar concern about activities that might be appealing or unappealing to *girls*. There have been many times when I have introduced Lego into a classroom situation, for example, and not thought twice about whether some of the girls might be turned off, at least at the outset. And I also thought, as I introduced this activity, that I would have to work harder at helping the children recognise and articulate the mathematics involved – something I would have been less aware of had we chosen to explore gears using Lego. (After all, that is engineering and construction, right? And there must be lots of maths in there – even if I cannot articulate it easily either.)

Terri, one of my BEd students at the University of British Columbia spoke eloquently about this issue in a paper she wrote describing her thoughts as she learned to crochet a blanket for her young toddler. A major undertaking I had assigned to my university maths students was to ask them to engage in something they had never done before – to learn about something new, taking notes as they went along and reflecting on the learning involved.

This assignment was called the 'personal project' – personal because the choice was entirely in the hands of the students, and a project, because the work was to extend over several months. People chose a variety of projects – learning to knit, making a cribbage board, ballroom dancing, making stained glass, woodworking, making twig furniture, learning to bake bread, pottery, making wine, print making, photography development and learning to fly an aeroplane (some personal projects gave 'risk-taking in teaching and learning' a whole new meaning).

Many students, at the beginning, could not imagine that their project would involve much mathematics beyond a bit of estimation and basic computation, but were delighted that they could count this kind of work as a maths assignment (a subject area that is dreaded by many beginning teachers). As their work unfolded, and we helped each other articulate the maths in the various projects, students were overwhelmed by the mathematics their work required. And some students, like Terri, began to see themselves as mathematicians, confronting issues of gender. Terri wrote:

> When I was thinking about what I would do for my personal project and [Rena] mentioned in class the option of knitting, I immediately thought 'where is the maths in that?'. As I started to crochet my baby's blanket I began to see what [she was] talking about. To crochet this blanket I had to use measurement skills for size, geometry and spatial sense for design, number sense and numeration for counting each stitch and [for] length of each crocheted square, patterns and relationships in order to produce an aesthetically [pleasing] pattern, design, and shape for the blanket, estimation to consider how much wool it would use, and the list could go on forever.
>
> [This project] made me realise how much maths we use in everyday life. It made me feel, and now here comes my quasi-feminist statement, how

undervalued many things have been in the past. Sewing, crocheting, and knitting were traditionally thought of as 'women's work' ... [the project] showed me how many skills, especially mathematical [ones], women possessed and were traditionally considered incapable of possessing. My maternal Grandmother taught me how to knit and sew when I was a small child. I do not think my Grandmother realised she possessed a number of maths skills in order to make her crafts; I think these skills were viewed by her and most people as 'real-world realities', as something you just knew.

(Haines, 1993, pp. 1–2)

The issues raised by Terri are echoed in the work of Lave (1988, 1991). You may recall Bill's reference, in the previous chapter, to Lave's account of situated cognition. This is precisely the kind of situated context referred to by Lave.

Another issue that surfaced in the making of paper jewellery was the role of tools. I have written about tools in other contexts, particularly with respect to traditional and computer tools for music composition (Upitis, 1992).[6] The two features of tools that I am especially interested in are their aesthetic appeal and their ability to be used by people with differing skill levels and for remarkably different purposes. Both of these issues came to mind as I watched Jennifer using my hammer to nail a hole into a piece of corrugated cardboard (see Figure 4.2).

It gave me pleasure to observe her concentration as she carefully held the nail in place so that her earring would have a hole in the right spot for the wire. I was thinking about how much I loved that hammer – it is quite old and well-made, with a strong wooden handle that is as smooth as a soapstone sculpture. I found myself remembering the forts of my childhood, and the time I spent using that hammer on a really large fort – my house. I then drifted to more recent uses – building an outhouse, a shed, and a cabin on a piece of wild land I purchased not so long ago.

I must have had a dreamy look in my eyes, because Jennifer asked me what I was thinking about. When I told her I was thinking about my outhouse, she rolled her eyes – that look that children give when they are pleased to be sharing a moment when their teacher is in a slightly crazy mood. Our conversation continued; I told Jennifer that I was going to build some twig furniture with that hammer, and we talked about how I would have to measure the trees and make sure the seat was the right height from the ground.

Outhouses and furniture and baby blankets are a long way from paper jewels. But if we are to design mathematics curricula and projects that make the learning of mathematics relevant and inclusive for all children, then I am convinced that personal projects like the ones I have described have an important part to play in the development of elementary mathematics.

Figure 4.2 Jennifer using a hammer

EILEEN

Many years ago I worked as a park director. It was a good way to make money in the summer between university terms. It also put me in close contact with children. I never thought any of the activities I did as a 'parkie' would show up in my maths classes. But paper necklaces did. As a parkie, I had to think up cheap activities for craft time each day that all the children could manage reasonably successfully. If the activity failed, I spent much of the remainder of the day picking up abandoned products.

I used to show the children how they could roll long strips of triangular-shaped paper into beads for necklaces. Magazines were my most common source material. I never even thought about the maths. I used only isosceles triangles, not because I wanted symmetrically curved beads, but because they were the first shape I tried. Both the summer children and I were pleased with the results.

When Rena and I were discussing maths projects and deciding what to try next, I was not surprised (would I ever be surprised again, after working with Rena for a year?) when she asked me what I thought about making jewellery.

I knew that if Rena suggested something it was worth considering. My mind raced as I thought about how I could incorporate the mathematics we had been exploring during the year into the making of necklaces, brooches, pins, earrings, and bracelets. How could mathematical concepts be used in jewellery making?

The first day we were planning this project, Rena brought along some samples of jewellery that she had made with other children over the years. I recognised many of the earrings she had worn during the time I had known her. Beautiful, bright, and looking like they had been purchased in a boutique along Vancouver's Fourth Avenue (outrageous and funky and at times monstrously expensive), I found out how incredibly simple they were in design – just pieces of paper rolled and twisted together. We looked at the shapes and I labelled them, untwisted them in my mind, and tried mentally constructing them in a new way.

Once again, mathematics was altering my vision. I began to look at jewellery ads differently. I no longer looked at the sparkling gems and glistening metals as my sole focus. Now I looked at shapes – both finished shapes, and shapes that I imagined were there initially, in two dimensions. This reminded me of my experience with tessellations, when previously unobserved maths started popping out at me from unexpected places. With jewellery, I looked at size changes and thought about scale transformations; I looked at shapes and thought about geometric combinations, and I looked at pleasing designs and thought of symmetry and balance.

Paper jewellery was planned as a whole-class project, right from the start. Both groups had a good grounding in the mathematics of tessellations, symmetry, and geometric shapes. These concepts are necessary to appreciate the activity and to develop the project as an application of mathematics. Also, Rena and I felt it would be fun to plan a project together, instead of pursuing related but separate projects as we had with the animation described in the previous chapter and string art in the next.

Besides the mathematics, there were a few other areas that needed to be explored prior to actually constructing our own jewellery. I was part of the learner group. Rena showed us how to twist wire effectively and safely. She spoke about combining not only different shapes, but different textures too. The sandpaper earrings really appealed to me. The term 'findings', used to describe the purchased bits of metal that would be needed (like earring hooks and brooch backs), was introduced.

Rena also talked to us about seeing things in new ways. Looking was not good enough. *Looking* was too passive; *seeing* implied active involvement. We saw how the same piece of paper was changed by a slight rotation or a flip. She encouraged us to spend a lot of time working with our materials, searching for the best perspective and most pleasing balance.

The day we actually made the jewellery was filled with anticipated pleasure. Even the few boys who had initially held back their enthusiasm were raring to go. Some of the children had decided to make something for themselves, some had decided to please a 'woman in their life' (mother, aunt, or sister), and some did not know who they would make their jewellery for, deciding to wait until they saw the finished product. One boy, in particular, was really ready. He knew exactly what he wanted to do, but was keeping it to himself – for the moment.

The children helped us place paper, all previously used and from various sources (described by Rena earlier in the chapter), in the middle of the open space in the room. Rena set out her bin of findings and beads and bits of 'junk', and we strung up our drying line. I talked to the children about the need to share and reminded them about safe behaviour with wire cutters, scissors, hammers, nails, and sharp pins. We also discussed moving carefully so we would not be the cause of someone's ruined project. (I soon realised nothing would be ruined. Things could always be reused in another way.)

It was apparent from the start that this was going to be an 'easy' project from the point of view of co-operation, common sense, and involvement. As teacher, my role seemed to be one of encourager, mediator in the learning experiences, and finder of the requested bits of material. I was also a learner. But I was clearly not needed to control behaviour or suggest ideas. I could walk around and genuinely appreciate the quality of work I observed. I use the term 'work' in this case both as an action and an object.

What of the boy who had his project mentally finished before we even started? Hardeep was, and to my knowledge still is, a *Star Trek* connoisseur. He wrote scripts for future shows in his Writer's Folder and built models of the ships in his free time. Not surprisingly, he decided to make a *Star Trek* communicator badge for his maths project.

Watching him was fascinating. He tried different stiffnesses of paper before deciding on a light corrugated cardboard. Then he had to find something that would cut through the cardboard. Next he experimented with size – size not only of each piece, but relative sizes as well. The *Star Trek* pin is made up of a silver oval shape with a gold concave quadrilateral positioned on top. Once it was obvious what Hardeep was making, nearly all of the boys wanted to make one.

Once the children were underway, I had the chance to put something together for myself. I decided to make a large brooch, using a combination of tissue paper and sandpaper. I cut out an irregular pentagon from light paperboard and covered it with dark blue tissue. Next, I cut out an equilateral triangle, slightly smaller than the pentagon, and covered it with purple tissue. Finally, I cut an isosceles triangle slightly smaller than the previous shape, from sandpaper, and coloured it gold. I spent a long time combining these shapes.

The children made decisions much faster than I did. Eventually, I made my choice, glued the pieces together, fastened a pin on the back, and went to the dipping room (coatroom, actually). It was a great feeling, not only to have made something that I enjoyed making and would continue to get pleasure from, but also to work co-operatively with the children in my class. I loved hearing their suggestions and encouragement as I worked on my piece, and found myself eagerly seeking advice from those children whose own work I admired.

Was my piece the best? Did it outshine the others? No – I needed more experience. My brooch gave me pleasure, but artistically, it lacked imaginative depth. Some of the children's pieces were much more striking than mine. Many made jewellery that jostled the senses. Some of their items were true gems of artistic and mathematical talent. Tracey exclaimed, while looking at her creation: 'I knew it would be good, but I never thought it would be *this* good'.

While writing the description of my brooch, I was once again aware of the amount of mathematics involved in this project. The next time I do it, I may ask the children to write a description of their jewellery pieces. I often ask children to make journal entries about maths.

For example, they describe how they figure something out, tell me how they are feeling about a new process, write problems for others or for themselves to solve, or predict how successful they will be on a worksheet. Writing about the thought processes of making jewellery and about the learning experience, in mathematical terms, would have been a wonderful way to close the project. I wish I had thought of it sooner. Experience, the great teacher.

This project lends itself well to other extensions. Often a class finds that it needs to raise money for a special trip, or for a school-wide fund raiser. Selling paper jewellery would be a great idea. Think of the mathematics involved in estimating and determining overall material costs, deciding on a profit margin, and promoting the products. Then there is the layout of the ads, scheduling of the selling, giving change, and keeping track of the money earned. The children could really run with this one.

If the class wanted to start the project by making paper as an initial activity, even more issues of recycling and mathematics could be drawn upon. What combinations of original paper sources produce the best ratio for jewellery paper? How can paper be pressed into jewellery shapes during its formative stage, just prior to drying? The children would be able to generate so many ideas to explore (children, the great teachers). This is problem solving at its best.

Real life – real problems – real solutions – real jewellery – real involvement – real maths.

BILL

Eileen was clearly taken with Rena's distinction between looking and seeing. Her observations of how she came to see just how much mathematics underpinned many aspects of the paper jewellery activity speaks eloquently to her point about experience being a master teacher. An auditory parallel can obviously be made to this visual image by thinking of the difference between listening and hearing. The importance of this sort of focused attention in contributing to the overall quality of an individual's life has been noted by the American psychologist Ellen Langer (1989) in her book *Mindfulness*.

A similar perspective has been outlined by Martin Mayeroff (1972) in his book *On Caring*. One of the most telling criticisms of contemporary education is that so many pupils seem to spend much of their time, at least while in school, in some sort of emotional and intellectual fog. They look and listen but neither see nor hear. At a time when human integrity seems under assault from both socio-economic instabilities and technological progress, it would seem essential that educational endeavours help develop an attitude of interest in, caring for, and understanding of, some of the manifold aspects of human experience.

There are, I think, at least two significant reasons why Rena has found the jewellery-making activity such a satisfying one over the years. From an emotional standpoint, it is something which she identifies strongly with; the original idea was hers, and it is an exercise which has become part of her shared experience with many individuals. Note the parallel here between Rena's experience and that of Doug, the young learner who described himself in a previous chapter as having 'discoverded' a tessellating quadrilateral pattern.

Both ideas were original in that neither Rena nor Doug had experienced their ideas before. But neither original idea was unique. Other people make paper jewellery, and did before Rena began crafting her own. Other people have tessellated quadrilaterals as well, long before Doug discovered his pattern. Original ideas – or non-derivative ideas – can be powerful even if not unique.

This notion is explored at length by Harvard professor Eleanor Duckworth (1987) in her book *The Having of Wonderful Ideas and Other Essays on Teaching and Learning*. In the lead essay, Duckworth describes her experience with a seven-year-old boy named Kevin. When she presented Kevin with a series of straws of different lengths, Kevin picked them up and said:

'I know what I'm going to do', and proceeded, on his own, to seriate them by length. He didn't mean, 'I know what you're going to ask me to do'. He meant, 'I have a wonderful idea about what to do with these straws. You'll be surprised by my wonderful idea'. . . . The having of wonderful ideas is what I consider to be the essence of intellectual development. And I consider it the essence of pedagogy to give Kevin the occasion to have his wonderful ideas and to let him feel good about himself for having them.

(p. 1)

Making paper jewellery, for Rena, was a wonderful idea.

Another attraction of the paper jewellery enterprise is that it requires making with one's hands. From a cognitive perspective, the dialectic between hand and brain is very potent. In a recent interview (Tomkins, 1994), the prominent contemporary Italian architect, Renzo Piano, observed that:

> A separation between knowing and understanding – or more precisely, between thinking and doing – has afflicted the practice of architecture for a long time. This separation between thinking and doing appears in all artistic disciplines, but in our field it is a catastrophe. ... It generates incompetence, because the cognitive and technical feedback that comes from doing is lacking. ... For me, architecture is a craft ... the making and the thinking are not separate.
>
> (p. 56)

The remarks of this distinguished architect are similar in many ways to positions articulated by some of the participants in the on-going debate about the merits of a 'constructivist' foundation for educational practice (Davis, Maher and Noddings, 1990). An even better fit is with the theories of Seymour Papert, whose book *Mindstorms: Children, Computers and Powerful Ideas* (1980) has been widely cited in educational computing circles.

The public reception of the Logo computer language (a language which had been described by Papert in this book) focused almost exclusively on a watered-down version (turtle graphics) of one, admittedly exceptionally powerful, application (turtle geometry) of this very potent computer language. In a parallel exercise at a more general level, discussion of Papert's ideas about mathematics, children, powerful ideas, and education were lost in the hyped, high-tech, rush to be seen to be using computers (Higginson, 1984; Papert, 1985).

Perhaps not since the days of John Dewey has public education had, in Papert, as powerful and versatile an intellect reflecting carefully on educational problems. (Papert, who now holds the Lego chair for Learning Research at MIT's Media Laboratory, was formerly Professor of Mathematics and co-director of the Artificial Intelligence Lab at the same institution, and before that was for four years a colleague of Jean Piaget at the University of Geneva.) One of his 'underdiscussed' ideas was that of 'objects to think with'. In the foreword Papert wrote to one of Rena's earlier books, he put it this way:

> Understanding learning is my lifelong passion. I have pursued it in many ways. I have read solemn theoretical treatises. I have even made theories of my own. But interestingly I find that what helps most is not the proliferation of abstract principles. I gain more by extending my collection of excellent 'learnings' – concrete learning situations that I can use as

'objects to think with.' And of such gems there is no richer source than Rena's work.

(Upitis, 1990a, pp. ix–x)

Like Rena, I have found paper to be a wonderful medium for the creation of 'objects to think with'. My approach is to use (recycled) paper to construct geometric objects. I will briefly describe one of these exercises in the context of work with a class of prospective mathematics teachers to make a few points. It is an exercise in constructing a truncated tetrahedron (think of slicing a layer off the bottom of a triangular pyramid and throwing away the top part) from a circular piece of paper. The steps are relatively easy to follow, particularly as the students are able to observe (hopefully see) what other individuals in the group are doing. The material is simple, the instructions straightforward and the number of mathematical concepts which emerge as the process unfolds is impressively large.

This, of course, is one of the reasons for drawing pupils' attention to this exercise in the first place. About halfway through this exercise an equilateral triangle appears. By folding one of its three vertices to the mid-point of the opposite side, a 'special' four-sided polygon is created. It is, in fact, a luxury model quadrilateral; one pair of sides being parallel with the shorter of those sides having a length a half of the other, and with the other pair of sides being equal in length. I enquire delicately as to whether anyone might know the name of such a beast.

A veteran of such inquisitions, I am braced for awkward silence and signs of discomfort; on occasions a brave soul might venture a highly tentative 'rhombus?'. Further questioning usually prompts admissions that some of them may have met such an object in their dimly remembered school daze. The term 'trapezoid' is acknowledged with little affection and its qualifying 'isosceles' with even less.

On occasion, I have had the somewhat cruel option of asking whether such things exist in the 'real worlds' of my charges. This always prompts a universally negative response, even on occasions when every student in the room is sitting at a table which has precisely (for very good combinatorial reasons) the shape in question. To say it again, we live in a culture where we very often look but do not see, and by so doing, we diminish daily the potential richness of our lives.

Rena also has a fascination for tetrahedra, and by now it should come as no surprise that her explorations would take on a larger and more dramatic form than those I have just described. When Rena returned to Ontario, one of her course assignments with pre-service teachers turned out to be the methods course on Elementary School Mathematics. In that context, she and her students built a 20-foot high tetrahedron, constructed entirely from newspaper dowels and masking tape.

The structure was remarkable – it was, in essence, a three-dimensional

Sierpinski fractal (see Chapter 6). Beginning with a large number (64, but who is counting) of tetrahedra made by joining six pieces of dowelling, each of these small tetrahedra was joined with one another, with each set of four tetrahedra forming a larger tetrahedron cluster. These four-tetrahedron clusters became the building blocks for the next level, as four of these were clustered in turn. The resulting structure was large enough for the entire class to fit inside.

These pre-service teachers were so excited by their work – and by their understanding of triangles, tetrahedra, structures, fractals, exponents, patterns, and the like – that one of them called the local newspaper (see Figure 4.3). A photographer and reporter arrived in short order; the students remained for almost two hours after the class had 'officially' ended to marvel at their structure and discuss how they could do the same activity with the children they would soon teach.

Having explored some of the attractions of making objects, having wonderful ideas, and the importance of having 'objects to think with', I now turn to a puzzling paradox.

A puzzle – and a game?

When Rena and I talk, we seldom disagree about priorities for education and for worthwhile ways for people to spend their time. It came as a jolt, therefore, when I first heard about Rena's distaste for games and puzzles.

Figure 4.3 Newspaper-dowel tetrahedron

These are things I enjoy, and feel are potentially rich for education. This makes me wonder why it is the case that all of Rena's examples of significant or real mathematics-making are bound up in the making of artifacts. Perhaps this is because Rena's view of puzzles and games ends with playing the games. By contrast, inherent in my vision of puzzles is the ultimate aim of creating one's own puzzles. I try to understand why games and puzzles work as they do, and get great satisfaction from designing variations on the puzzles and games I encounter.

The topic of games comes up in Eileen's discourse and experience as well. Eileen noted in Chapter 1 that when she moved from the use of manipulatives and maths projects to more traditional forms of mathematics teaching, she could not sustain the textbook paper-and-pencil methods without adding maths games as a regular component of her programme. As soon as she reinstated a maths games period into her programme, she felt better immediately. In subsequent conversations with Eileen, I have learned that one reason she reinstated the games was that she herself enjoyed them. The other, of course, was that her pupils thrived when a regular time to play maths games was introduced.

Eileen, therefore, does not share Rena's distaste for games. But like me, Eileen's use of games includes the creation of new games. As part of her involvement with the E-GEMS (*Electronic Games for Education in Mathematics and Science*) project,[7] Eileen observed her pupils playing games, and then had them design board games of their own. The second issue is that part of Rena's distaste for games is her association of games with what she regards as harmful in the popular culture of children – television (with its game shows), video and computer games, and media violence in general.

Where does this leave us? In attempting to make sense of this, I realised that Rena's passion for music had many similarities with my feeling for games. Both of us have spent many hours absorbed by our passions. How did our respective experiences with games and music evolve? Arguably, we began at the same stage – that of *ignorance*. Having being introduced, at an early age in both cases, to the activities, we began to participate by following the rules – what I have come to see as the stage of *compliance*. In other words, I learned to follow the instructions of my peers as they introduced me to the various games of childhood.

I vividly remember playing cards as a child. When I was eight, my friends and I created our own version of a casino in my parents' garage, as we spent an entire summer playing *War*, *Go Fish*, and *Crazy Eights*. When Rena was eight, she was learning the rules of music – playing simple pieces on the piano while learning to read standard music notation. In both cases, the introduction was positive: when I learned about games and when Rena learned about music, neither of us developed an early aversion to these activities. I was introduced to music at this age as well, but disliked my piano teacher, did not like to practice, and when I hit middle C so hard that the piano broke, my mother gave up on her somewhat unrealistic ambition of having a piano virtuoso for a son.

As the years passed, despite occasional episodes of indifference or even aversion, the compliance Rena and I associated with music and games, respectively, evolved to a higher level, one of understanding or *cognisance* of the richness of the activities. Instead of merely following the rules of a game or playing the music on the page, we both became cognisant of the underlying structures of certain game types and musical genres. I became attracted to a class of games based on word manipulation, including *Scrabble* and *Boggle*. In a parallel way, Rena explored the work of Baroque and Romantic composers, leaving, for the moment, the Classical composers and Impressionists behind.

Again, over a period of time, our understanding deepened and our level of personal involvement increased to the extent that we became *creators* in our respective areas. Rena began to shape music in new ways; as a performer, she became an interpreter of music rather than ending with note reading (compliance) or understanding structures (cognisance). As a composer, she began to create original works, using the understanding of structure and form she had developed earlier.

In my case, variations on themes began to emerge. I made new games, based on others that I had both played (compliance) and understood (cognisance), games which were original and personally meaningful. In some important ways, then, we were shaping our fields and our fields were helping to define us as individuals. This shaping occurred not in a twenty-minute lesson, but over many years of involvement. This pattern invites reflection on what usually happens in school settings.

Eight-year-olds have already had experiences that have moved them from ignorance to the early stages of compliance, if they have not taken a road leading to aversion or indifference. The sad thing is that schools are almost always structured so that compliance is seen as the endpoint in intellectual enquiry – at least in mathematics. Texts are the holy books of compliance. With a few notable exceptions, most textbooks set up a model for grading which is based on how closely the pupil follows the rules. Cognisance and creation, in the form of understanding and changing the rules, seldom emerge from school activities.

This is probably understandable, given the large number of teachers who have never passed the level of compliance themselves. It is also understandable, given the production or industrial model of schooling as described by Franklin (1990) where the production of uniform products is the desired outcome and fundamental aim of the enterprise. Introducing cognisance or creation threatens standard outcomes. Not only is mathematics taught as an exemplar of production mentality, but as its archetype.

Mathematics, as it is typically presented, cuts people off from their local environment – this is the essence of abstraction and compliance. It is a particularly damaging model for girls and women, for research has shown that girls and women value relationships and connections and contextualisation for their learning (Belenky, Clinchy, Goldberger, and Tarule, 1986).

This is not to say that teachers always hinder growth beyond compliance. Returning to our experiences, Rena arguably never passed the stage of compliance with games. Why not? And why did I not become engaged by music? Rena's music experiences, unlike mine, were filled with outstanding teachers. The reason they were outstanding was that they combined caring with the expectation that she had the capability to advance much further, possibly even past their own level of cognisance or creation. Obviously, this was not the relationship I had with my music teacher. But I had good 'game teachers' – my peers, my family, and the characters in the books I read.

It is no accident, therefore, that my views of mathematics are strongly influenced by the intrigue of language and its structures, just as Rena's views of mathematics are informed by her musical soul. Contrast this view of integration – long to evolve, widely influenced, coupled with social interactions, and strongly tied to one's sense of self – with the sums on orange pumpkin-shaped paper mentioned in the previous chapter.

Games in educational settings

Given the foregoing analysis, we have to examine carefully what is offered in educational settings to children under the label of 'game'. What we wish to avoid are those games which allow no latitude for creation or appropriation or modification in some form – games that are inherently limited to *compliance*. Today's youth spend a good deal of time playing games that are limited to compliance. I am thinking here of the plethora of video and computer games that have flooded the commercial markets and occupy many hours of children's lives. Even if the games were not filled with graphic violent images and the depiction of highly questionable and limiting roles for women, the fundamental principle of most video games is to kill or be killed. There is no room for modification of this simple, black and white, plot.

As Provenzo (1991) writes: 'In the case of Nintendo the child has almost no potential to reshape the game and its instrumental logic. There is literally one path down which the player can proceed' (p. 137). And further:

> The enemy is anonymous. There is no understanding of why things are the way they are – no history, no context, simply a threat and the need to act ... [the player] must assume the role of being either good or evil. There are no shades of grey in the world of Nintendo.
>
> (pp. 126–7)

How does the time that children spend playing video games outside of school affect their use and judgement of technology in school, technology that is often quite different from the video games? In a paper from the E-GEMS group, where the use of computers and video games within and outside a Grade 7/8 classroom was documented over a school year, it was observed by the researchers that pupils judged computer software on the basis of standards they used to judge video games, standards that were often inappropriate for the computer software they were examining (DeJean and Upitis, 1995).

Further, most of the Grade 7 and 8 boys in the class were, or had been, avid video game players, and this made them more comfortable with other forms of technology – the technology they found in the classroom. It would appear that there is something to Provenzo's claim that video games are: 'an important entryway into the world of computing' (1991, p. 117). Is this yet another way that girls become marginalised from technology?

Then there is the issue of violence. Video games represent 'neither a neutral nor a trivial technology, [but are] redefining the symbolic under-pinnings of our culture' (Provenzo, 1991, p. 33). In a society where the popular culture depicts women as weak and subservient, or alternately, as evil vixens, what roles are girls to model? What roles will boys expect girls and women to play?

In a recent doctoral dissertation, where hundreds of studies examining the role of media violence over the past three or four decades were analysed, Dyson (1995) reached the undeniable conclusion that media violence has led to a more violent culture. She demonstrated how television has been linked to reduced attention spans, crankiness or misbehaviour, hyperactivity, and lazy reading (Dyson, 1995; Radecki, 1990; Winn, 1977). She quotes Radecki, a child psychiatrist and research director of NCTV, who claims that the evidence that TV violence has a harmful effect on viewers is as strong as the evidence that cigarettes cause lung cancer (Radecki, 1990, p. 1).

Dyson makes direct links between the violence of television and the violence of video games, showing how one reinforces the other. In a call for urgent shifts in media programming, she noted that the

> Need for these shifts is underscored in the widespread recognition that communications technology on a global basis is converging and subse-quently propelling us along a new 'information superhighway'. . . . I have argued that the . . . highway needs a few rules of the road.

> (p. 289)

One way to counter the negative influence of video games and other forms of popular media is to move from compliance to cognisance and creation. Some of the Grade 7/8 boys described earlier reached a stage where they started creating their own video games (Saxton and Upitis, 1995). Not only did this allow the game creators to move beyond compliance, but it afforded opportunities for the researchers – one of whom was Rena – to talk with them as they created their games, offering a critical perspective on the video game culture while at the same time supporting their creative endeavours.

In one of the research reports, Rena described how Matt created a standard video game and then began to reflect on how that game could be modified to change the stereotypically set gender roles. I quote here from her paper:

> Matt's game, *Puzzle Castle*, was a major undertaking. ... He described spending '*hours* on the game – lots. Every period at school, I would work on the game'. ... When asked to describe his game, Matt replied, 'It's about a knight who has to save a princess. He has to solve problems to free the princess, basically. Maths problems and riddles'....
>
> [When I saw the game, I asked] Matt if it were possible for [the princess] – a woman – to be the hero. Matt replied that he had never thought of that, but eagerly responded with a suggestion: 'At the start, I could ask, please enter your gender. They could have the same story and riddles, but wherever it said "princess" it would say "prince"'. When asked if he had ever seen a game like that, he replied that he hadn't. He then was asked to think about whether a game like his, with a gender option, would sell. He seemed to think it would, responding, 'Yeah, unless it was a really boring game. It would probably sell better. If some people felt stereotyped about games, like heroes as men and distressed damsels and stuff, then more girls would buy it, maybe.'
>
> (pp. 14–16)

How, then, should we examine computer-based classroom tools, given the context of the popular culture? How can mathematics technology compete with the technology of the popular culture? What cultural messages are we sending about mathematics against the larger cultural backdrop I have just painted?

A character in one of Kurt Vonnegut's novels remarks in a reflective moment that 'we are what we pretend to be, therefore we should be careful what we pretend to be'. Yoked to Marshall McLuhan's most famous epigram, 'the medium is the message', and set in a mathematics teaching context, the lesson would seem to be that we should be careful what tools (media) we use in mathematics classrooms because they may well determine the essential nature of the experience for pupils.

This is perhaps especially true of computer-based tools. Three different pieces of mathematics software, two of which I have already discussed (*Tesselmania!* and Logo), and a third, *Counting on Frank* (developed in part through consultation with the E-GEMS group) are each, in their own way, a classic of their type. Each is thoroughly planned, implemented with care and professionally presented. In keeping with the genre, they all require a high level of initial compliance – poor spelling and inaccurate keyboarding are not tolerantly received.

Counting on Frank was designed to embed some mathematical concepts in the context of what the designers and researchers hoped would become an attractive game for children. It is the easiest of the three to use. Charming cartoon-like figures lead the player through the game where the object is to guess the number of jelly beans in a jar in order to win a trip to Hawaii. Clues are collected as standard word problems are solved. Not coincidentally, *Counting on Frank* is also the most limited in its potential. *Tesselmania!* occupies the middle ground. It invites cognisance and permits a somewhat restricted version of creativity. Learners can create some quite attractive artifacts, but within narrowly defined bounds (see Chapter 2 for a fuller discussion of this tool).

Logo is the most ambitious of the three. It demands cognisance and strongly encourages creativity. Its heritage – it is a sibling of Lisp, one of the most powerful computer languages ever created – means that the scope for creativity is exceptionally wide. The trade-off for this is that the teacher needs to know a great deal before she or he can begin to realise this potential. Given that a similar statement could be made about almost any significant human activity – consider music, for example – the reception of Logo by the educational community seems somewhat naive.

By contrast, in the world of children's traditional games and pastimes, there is room for creativity (Opie, 1969). While the different game types remain fixed across cultures and time, individual games are modified from one setting to another depending on the number of children present or on the existence of particular features in the local environment. My favourite 'localisation' (which I suspect may be apocryphal) is that of the classic (and exceptionally rich from a mathematical perspective) activity of 'paper, stone and scissors'.

In parts of Africa this reputedly becomes elephant, anteater, and earwig. The equivalence of the two games might puzzle one at first until it is understood that earwigs can crawl in one ear of the elephant and out the other to devastating pachydermal effect. In mathematical games, creativity in the form of 'variations on a theme' is the quintessence of the enterprise as Berlekamp, Conway and Guy have shown in their magisterial, two-volume work, *Winning Ways for Your Mathematical Plays* (1982).

The challenge, it would appear, is to design and to help children design mathematical games that have the timelessness of 'paper, stone, and scissors', the appeal of the video games of the popular culture, the laudable story-line and humour of *Counting on Frank*, the creative potential of Logo, and the accessibility of *Tesselmania!*. An impossible task, perhaps. But better that this task be in the hands of teacher-researchers like Rena and Eileen and their E-GEMS collaborator Maria Klawe than in the hands of textbook creators or programmers of video games.

Chapter 5

Kaleidoscopes and composition
'Are we doing cemetery again today?'

EILEEN

'Cemetery!' exclaimed Amber loudly and incredulously: 'we're going to study cemeteries in maths!'

'No, Ms. Phillips said we're going to explore Symemitry.'

'That's right, but I already know about symmetry. We made folded paper cut-outs in Grade 3 or Grade 2, I can't remember which. Symmetry means both sides are the same.'

'Cemeteries are full of dead people.'

'Symmetry means ... like you're looking in a mirror.'

'I've done symmetry. It's boring. Can't we do something else?'

All I had done was write the word SYMMETRY in large capital letters across the small amount of board space which existed in my room. (Not that there is anything wrong with blackboards, but there was so little visible storage space that I tended to cover the boards with displays and ongoing projects.) Most of the Grade 4s had reacted with excitement, some trying to understand the term, some trying to say the word, and some trying to recount their previous experiences. In this case, merely writing the topic word was enough to provide me with feedback about the levels of readiness of my pupils. No need for a formal pre-test.

This is going to be very interesting, perhaps somewhat challenging, I thought. Even though it is usual to have a wide range of prior knowledge going into a new classroom topic, I felt this spread was wider than most. There were some pupils who could not even pronounce the word, some who felt they were experts, and many who were in between. And then, there was me; I would also be a learner in this search for, and about, symmetry.

I was immediately curious about what Amber's reaction would be when she found out that we would not be exploring cemeteries for examples of symmetry. Amber was the type of divergent thinker who would probably have done very well if much of her mathematics were presented in a graveyard. She would have enjoyed the computations involved in finding how old people were when they died, comparing relative gravestone sizes, and searching for symmetry within and amongst the tombstones.

Another pupil, Darren, had written in his journal that he really wanted to use some more mathematical tools. I felt that a protractor might appeal to him and that this would be an appropriate spot to present one. I was concerned about Kent who had already 'done' symmetry. Often an attitude of closure is hard to reopen. I hoped I could get his previous experience to work for me.

Both Carl and Arthur had done some wonderful work with line art (Figure 5.1), extending their work into extravagant designs, and I looked forward to seeing how their creative eyes and mathematical minds would play with symmetry.

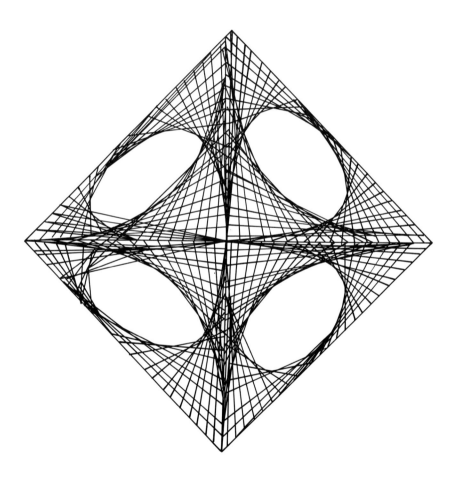

Figure 5.1 Arthur and Carl's line art

Loose strings

This line art work could be considered the beginning of the symmetry unit, though, at the time, it was seen as an end in itself. I knew that I wanted the children to experience geometry as more than the study of shapes and the memorisation of terms. I wanted them to recognise geometry as it is readily found in their lives – in the buildings around them, in nature, in print designs. Toward this end, we discussed architecture, we looked at transformations we could do on the computer, we studied patterns, we revisited tessellations, and we made nature prints. As the main maths project for this unit, my intention was for the class to make pictures using string. I have seen this referred to as *symmography* (Kreischer, 1971).

To begin, I introduced the class to co-ordinates on the x- and y-axes. They learned how to name line segments by referring to their end points, using both positive and negative numbers. Everyone made great line drawings and, as mentioned earlier, some were able to complete complex designs. All of the pupils were able to describe their designs using the symbols of the Cartesian co-ordinate system. In the past, I have had pupils who were able to make line drawings that were as complex as these, but who were only able to describe the process in terms of patterning. In contrast, the pupils this year spoke with considerable sophistication:

> 'For this quadrant I started my first segment at (–1,8); then I went to (–2,7), then to (–3, 6).'

> 'Well, I wanted to make my design over here. So, I put my ruler on the top mark going up and on the first mark to the left on this line. Then I connected them. Next I moved my ruler down one space and over one space, and connected them. I just continued until I had finished matching them all up.'

The resulting products from pupils over the years have looked the same, but the amount of mathematical understanding, as demonstrated through discussion, has been markedly different. This also demonstrates the importance of discourse in the teaching and learning of mathematics. Merely looking at the end product is not enough. It often surprises me that so many of my colleagues are still content simply to mark a computation as right or wrong, completely ignoring the importance of discussing the process. Or, if they do carry on a discussion, it is with those pupils who 'got it wrong'. Just as the two line segment drawings looked alike, that is, they were 'right', so too can two 'right' answers in computation be attained through different processes. It is always interesting to ask pupils with correct answers to explain what they did. In this way, assessment can be an ongoing process of observation and discussion.

To illustrate this point even further, I will relate an anecdote about my daughter. One day, when I picked up my then four-year-old daughter from her daycare, she presented me with a small scrap of paper. She seemed extremely pleased with herself and proud of this paper remnant. So, as mothers often do, I told her that it was wonderful, took it home, and put it on the fridge. I must admit, however, that to me it looked like a scrap for the recycling bin.

The next day as I arrived to pick her up she was busily working at the art centre. I went over to see what she was doing. She was carefully cutting a shape out of a folded piece of paper. When she opened the paper, she examined the results. She cut off the top part, refolded the paper, and cut again. She continued this process until all that was left was a tiny scrap. I could now see why she had been so enthusiastic the day before. This bit of paper was the culmination of many trials and represented all the cuttings and shapes and designs that had been pared away in her personal paper-cutting project. Observing the process gave me insight into what she was experimenting with and provided me with direction for intervention, had I chosen to mediate.

Now, back to the geometry sessions. After the pupils made their line drawings, they were to choose one to make using string and cardboard. I thought this would be a good step between working on paper and creating a complete picture using string. As they were doing this, I found myself feeling as if this were a closure, not a mid-point in an exploration. I was not looking forward to extending the project in the way that I had planned, that is, moving away from the string and cardboard to string with other media. The idea of making kaleidoscopes came to me one night. (Ideas often come to me between the hours of two and four in the morning – a time when sensible people are deeply asleep.)

Yes, kaleidoscopes would be a perfect project for symmetry and related concepts of geometry. I could use the string art as a bridge into a further study of symmetry that would be needed for the kaleidoscopes project to proceed with understanding. There would be no loose strings!

Another view of symmetry

I decided to begin explorations of symmetry with a playing-around stage. Using line symmetry as the focus, I drew a dotted line with a set of lines on one side.

Eileen: How would you complete this picture so that it is the same on both sides of the dotted line? I want it to be the same if I could fold this part of the board on top of this … sort of like folding paper.

Nathan: I'd go over your lines really dark and then I'd trace it. Then I'd make the tracing again on the other side.

Eileen: Can you do it for me? I'd like to see if it would work when we're doing our independent experimentation. I'll leave this drawing for you, O.K.?

As Nathan left, I wondered if he would complete the symmetry, by flipping the image he traced, or if he would slide the image over, repeating the image to make a pattern. Carl came up with another idea:

Carl: I'd use my ruler to measure the lines and then I'd make other ones exactly the same on the other side.

Eileen: I'd like to see you do that, but I've already said Nathan could use these lines. Is it alright if I make you a similar one to work from?

Carl: O.K.

And Rishma added:

Rishma: I'd just draw the lines on the other side. That would be close enough.

Eileen: I'll draw you a similar set of lines and let you try.

Eileen: [To the class] Before we begin our actual experimentation, I want all of you to have the chance to share your thinking. Turn to the person next to you and spend the next two minutes talking about how you would create a symmetrical pattern. Remember to talk and listen. I'll circulate and see what ideas I can hear.

All pupils had an opportunity to contribute an idea they thought would work. In addition to those related above, these included:

'I would get tracing paper and trace one side, then fold it over and trace again.'

'I would cut it out and then I could move it.'

'I'd fold the paper first and just cut any old shape. When I open it, I'd be finished.'

As you can see, we very quickly generated some ideas about creating pictures with line symmetry. For the balance of this period, the pupils experimented with paper, pencil, and rulers, to see whether they could create symmetrical designs. Some were more accurate than others, but they all demonstrated an understanding of line symmetry. I made a note to myself to have them work with partners in the next session, with lots of tools.

What is symmetry?

The second session started with the reading of *What is Symmetry?* (Sitomer and Sitomer, 1970). This book uses simple pictures to illustrate the concepts of line symmetry, point symmetry, and plane symmetry. Since I had some difficulty distinguishing between line and plane symmetry myself, I asked the children what they understood as the difference. The major one that we could agree on was that plane symmetry was like a reflection. However, we also discussed how the line where the reflection started could be seen as a line of symmetry. We agreed we would focus on line symmetry and point symmetry for this period. Like Rena, when she was only willing to go so far in her explorations of pentagons, I too was reluctant to extend the exploration past my level of comfort.

Using pattern blocks, tangram sets, and geoboards, I asked the pupils to demonstrate line and point symmetry. They were encouraged to work with a partner or in a group no larger than three.

This was almost *déjà vu*. Tessellations and line drawings re-emerged, this time under the guise of symmetry. Some of the pupils created patterns that contained both types of symmetry in one, others kept theirs separate. Often one pattern would have several lines of symmetry – horizontal, vertical, and diagonal (see Figure 5.2).

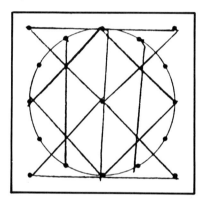

Figure 5.2 A geoboard pattern containing horizontal, vertical and point symmetry

Some of the drawings were complex patterns (see Figure 5.3), others were images that represented a real object.

All pupils were busy and talkative. They explained their drawings easily to each other and to me in terms of the symmetry they had created or discovered. I find that when children are genuinely exploring they share without fear of failure. They know that we are all learning together and realise the value of discussing their hypotheses and findings.

More tools

Some of the children were intrigued with the idea of measuring degrees of angles to create drawings that would be symmetrical. They easily grasped the way to use a protractor and decided to use rulers for measuring length. Sure, there were some miscalculations, but not misunderstandings. It was exciting

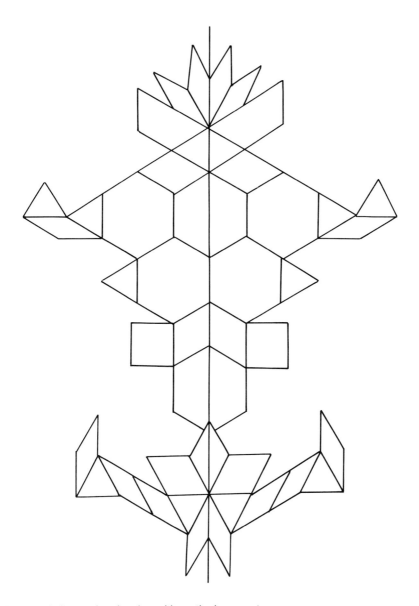

Figure 5.3 A complex drawing with vertical symmetry

to observe the children making sense of a new technique. What was immediately obvious was how well they used their mistakes to guide their learning. None of them was upset if something did not work; they made adjustments and kept on going.

It was interesting that the pupils who chose to use hand mirrors and a Mira opted to create drawings of things like people and horses (see Figure 5.4)

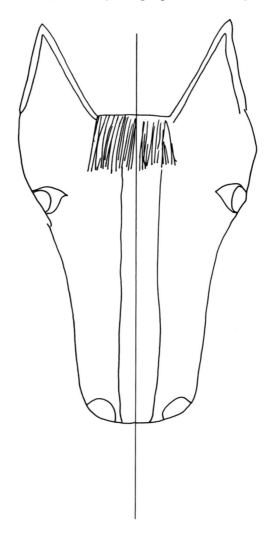

Figure 5.4 A drawing created using hand mirrors and the Mira

Those who chose to use protractors and rulers made drawings that contained only straight line segments (see Figure 5.5). This was not something that was taught, it was something that emerged from the choice of the tools themselves. I wondered if they had not had access to all of these tools whether their understanding would have been more limited. As it was, at the

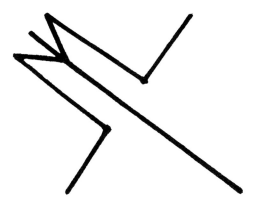

Figure 5.5 A drawing created using a ruler and a protractor

end of this session, we had a 'gallery showing'[8] and everyone had exposure to each of the symmetrical masterpieces that had been created. In the time between this session and the next, pupils often borrowed the tools for further explorations during their independent work time.

The promise of kaleidoscopes

Up to this time, I had kept the idea of making a kaleidoscope to myself. I did not want to excite the children and then not be able to follow through. When I first mentioned the idea of making kaleidoscopes to Rena, I confessed to her that I had always wanted to try making one, but had been reluctant for various reasons – the usual reasons: fear, expense, and lack of time. I told her I would go to our local science supply and bookstore and see what I could find.

The search resulted in the perusal of several expensive and complicated books and the eventual purchase of a cheap book of tricks with a simple kaleidoscope entry (Supraner, 1981). Rena, also, kept her eyes open and found a nature crafts book that contained a 'recipe' for a slightly more complicated kaleidoscope (Diehn and Krautwurst, 1992).

I decided that by using both of the methods offered (one using mirrors as the reflective surface and the other using acetate), it would be possible for each child to create a working kaleidoscope. I shared my new maths project idea with my Grade 4 group. I told them that we would be doing the mathematics that would lead up to the project and that they would have a chance to share their knowledge with the Grade 3 group so that we could each make a kaleidoscope. During this period I also had the group mentally follow the construction of the kaleidoscope models. I also asked them to generate a list of variables that could be used to create spin-off models and designs.

Here are some of their 'what would happen if?' ideas.

What would happen if you:

- coloured the acetate a different colour (not black, as suggested)?
- used an isosceles triangle (rather than an equilateral one)?
- used a pentagon or a hexagon?
- used a really wide triangle?
- made the prism short?
- made the prism long?
- left the acetate clear?
- coloured the end (rather than leaving it clear)?
- made a small eye-hole?
- made a large eye-hole?
- put your bits of paper in the middle?
- put your bits of paper at the corners?
- made your design symmetrical?
- made your design just 'fall loose'?

This was energising and a little overwhelming. I told the group to pay attention to any kaleidoscopes they came across and to think about how we might make our own. I had already told them we would be taking ideas from both examples, but that we would not follow either one exactly. In the meantime, our project was put on hold for awhile so we could lend a hand with the animation (see Chapter 3). There is a timeline of the school year in Appendix A which shows the relative sequence of the projects. It is possible that in this chapter the chronology of the different projects might begin to intrude, as many of the projects overlapped, and some were halted while another one took precedence which were subsequently returned to.

The break from symmetry turned out to be longer than we had expected due to a three-week teachers' strike in our school district. Rena and I both began to feel a little panicked as the end of May quickly approached. We felt a need for closure. In addition to this, I was beginning to prioritise all the things that would have to be done if we ever returned to class during the school year. There were many who were forecasting an October end to the strike.

On May 30, we returned to school. Time was really closing in on us, as term ended at the end of June. I had a student teacher working with me who needed to see an end to some of her units and I wanted to have time for kaleidoscopes. Rena and I also wanted to give the whole class the opportunity to celebrate their animation success with a full viewing of *The Changes*, complete with music and narration.

One session to practice

With time at a premium, I had to decide if it was worth following through with the kaleidoscope project. Perhaps it was enough that the children had played around with symmetry. Perhaps it was better not to do a rushed job.

It is difficult to know what would have been best, but I am pleased that I decided to go ahead and push the project through. Our schedule permitted one session to play with the materials before starting the construction of the kaleidoscopes. The class had a brief session during which the Grade 4s talked to the Grade 3s about their knowledge of symmetry. The Grade 3s were able to ask questions and then all the children were given several mirrors.

'I can count 18 reflections when I bring two mirrors close together.'

'I think it works best when the mirrors aren't too angled, but they should be closer than a right angle.'

'My mirrors reflect for ever and ever if you look at the right spot.'

'If you make them straight, they don't reflect at all.'

'I like it when you put the short ends together.'

At the end of this session, I really wondered if I had made the right decision in continuing. We had not even had a chance to try the acetate and many of the 'what if?' variables that had been suggested prior to the strike had not been explored. Because of the long break, some of the children seemed less sure of the vocabulary of symmetry than I would have preferred. I expected that terms like 'flips', 'slides', 'rotations', and 'lines of symmetry' would be part of each pupil's ready vocabulary. As it was, some of them were still thinking the terms through. They did, however, have an intuitive under-standing of what the terms meant and how the various transformations appeared. The class was keen and I decided we would make kaleidoscopes, using acetate, on the last Monday of the school year.

Kaleidoscopes it is!

Monday morning arrived. The pupils and I were anxious to dispense with the usual routine of attendance and get started. All the materials we would need were either in the centre of the room, in the recycling box near the window, or on the children's desks.

I had decided not to pre-cut or sort the materials that would be needed. This was in keeping with our other maths projects and with Rena's and my unspoken agreement that the children should do as much as possible themselves in order to achieve maximum growth and a feeling of ownership. As I write this I find it curious that she and I never felt the need to voice aloud our thinking on this aspect of the projects. It probably came up in a circuitous way, but I believe we instinctively knew this was the preferred way for both of us to work. It may sound strange to hear me reflecting on the importance of this, but I believe that the things that are taken for granted are of equal importance to the success of a project as the things that are minutely planned.

The children and I met on the carpet, reviewed the steps for making a standard kaleidoscope, discussed our time constraints, and decided on the size of our own kaleidoscopes. As soon as the pupils were ready, they each took a rectangle of light cardboard, an acetate strip cut from the end of an overhead projector roll, and a few pieces of masking tape. Working by sharing ideas with each other, each pupil busily set out to create his or her kaleidoscope. They moved about the classroom freely, getting more tape as needed, finding coloured paper to cut into bits, and seeing how others handled problems they were encountering. By noon, most of the children had completed their kaleidoscopes. Some needed a few more minutes and asked to eat in the room during lunch so they could finish. Each kaleidoscope was unique, just as each of our other projects had produced an individual, no-name-needed, product.

Our kaleidoscope 'recipe'

I have carefully considered this heading, as some may choose to make kaleidoscopes as a craft or fun project, rather than as a context for mathematical explorations – like baking a loaf of bread without under-standing the properties of flour and yeast. While perfectly acceptable, and still more delicious than the store-bought variety, what will be missing is the understanding of how the ingredients combine. Nevertheless, there are times when following a recipe best suits current needs, and experimenting with ingredients has to wait. This made me think of Bill's compliance, cognisance and creation categories.

Equipment

- one roll of overhead projector film
- felt pens (permanent markers)
- lightweight cardboard (similar to the weight of cracker boxes)
- tape
- scraps of coloured paper

Method

Because we lacked extensive time to experiment, we stayed with the traditional kaleidoscope's shape of a triangular prism. Each child decided on the length and diameter of the prism that he or she would build. Then they:

- cut the cardboard to the size chosen;
- cut the acetate to overlay one side of the cardboard strip (some coloured the acetate black, hoping to make it more reflective; others left it clear);
- taped acetate to cardboard;

- taped the acetate-covered strips together to form a triangular prism, shiny side in;
- cut out a triangular piece of cardboard to cover one end of the prism, and used a pencil to poke a hole through it for the eye piece;
- taped this triangular piece to the prism (some pupils taped this down by using the tape as a seam joiner; others made flaps on their end-pieces, and used tape to hold these in place);
- cut two acetate triangles for the other end. They then put scraps of coloured paper between the layers (there were many versions of this – some left the pieces to fall freely, some taped them in place: some formed a design with their pieces, some left them how they landed; all of them worked).

Closing thoughts

Although the kaleidoscopes session was rushed at the end, it was still a part of one of the longest projects, for our work on symmetry began long before the kaleidoscopes were constructed. Nevertheless, I would have liked the children to have had the opportunity to explore their 'what if?' variations, and I would build in the time needed for that sort of experimentation the next time around.

Symmetry – of various forms – seems to come naturally to children. I have already told of my young daughter, Jaclyn's, early explorations with symmetry when I discussed the importance of observing processes. Jaclyn soon realised she did not have to cut away and discard each piece after she finished cutting it. Once she discovered this, our house was filled with pictures and with faces and masks that she had folded and cut. Sometimes her folds would simply be halves, but more often they would be variations of quarters. Her favourite mask resulted from a piece of paper she had folded once vertically and then opened to fold each parallel edge into the centre before refolding the centre line – in this way, she was using both point and line symmetry. She would cut, unfold, view, and exclaim, 'Ah!' or 'Oh!', then refold and repeat the process.

When this masterpiece was finished she brought it to me with a special sense of accomplishment. We sat and studied it together for a long time and we talked about all of the parts that were the same. I decided to introduce her to the word 'symmetry' and was surprised when she readily repeated the word back to me. We found all her cut-out bits and paired them with their symmetrical partners. Then we took bits and arranged and rearranged them into several different symmetrical designs. Each time we identified the symmetry. Sometimes it was a vertical line, sometimes a horizontal or a diagonal one. A few days later, when we were reading one of Jaclyn's books, she said: 'Look, Mummy, there's some symmetry.' The picture was of Bambi looking at his reflection in the pond.

Whenever possible, it is desirable to build on children's intuitive understanding. Symmetry seems to be an area that calls on such understanding.
The concepts of geometric transformation are readily constructed by pupils
who have played around with symmetry. The language used to describe
transformations and symmetry is easily acquired in these circumstances.
Perhaps this is because they are learning a label that describes a concept they
already have experience with, rather than learning both a label and a new
concept simultaneously.

RENA

Eileen was not the only one who was surprised to see symmetry popping up
in various guises. Pictures of Bambi, arrangements of bathroom tiles, and
kaleidoscopes made with triangular prisms may not seem close relatives at
first glance. Even though I had been thinking about symmetry for years,
some of the 'real-world' examples surprised me as well. And now, I describe
the work I was doing with the Grade 3 pupils on music composition, work
that was closely linked to notions of symmetry and other mathematical
twists and transformations – a kaleidoscope of sound.

It has been noted for centuries that mathematics and music share many
common features: it is not unusual to find people who have interests and
skills in both disciplines. Composers have been known to use mathematical
patterns to create musical compositions. Similarly, mathematicians use the
regularities of art and music better to understand mathematical principles
(Kappraff, 1991; Peterson, 1990).

It certainly does not surprise me that mathematicians and musicians have
a lot in common. For years (but it feels like centuries) I have been interested
in the parallels between the two disciplines, especially in the context of
helping children improvise and compose music.

The specific composition project I describe in this chapter is one that I
have undertaken several times before. However, I had done this with high
school students in advanced geometry and algebra courses, with secondary
mathematics teachers, and with university students.[9] So I was a little unsure
as to how it would translate to the Grade 3 crowd. I need not have worried;
as the expression goes, they took to it like ducks to water.

The basic idea was a simple one. I began by drawing a cat in the upper
right corner on a piece of paper on a flip chart. I then asked the children how
I could transform or modify the cat without changing its basic shape. Jennifer
suggested that I could 'flip it' and draw it backwards. I did this, placing the
transformed cat to the left of the original (tried to, anyway, wondering why
I had started with a cat and not with something simpler). I then asked for
ideas. The pupils readily provided more possibilities, including an upside-
down cat, and an upside-down and backwards cat. They also identified the
translation – moving the cat to a different location without changing its

shape, and changes in size or scale, as indicated below.

Throughout our conversation, the children indicated that they were thinking about how all of this would become music.

> 'You could just move it.'
>
> 'Yes, that's called a translation.'
>
> 'Is that like translating something from English into French, but like it's still the same word?'
>
> 'Yes, that's exactly what it's like.'
>
> 'You could make it bigger or smaller, but it would still be the same shape.'
>
> 'Can we use half notes and everything for this?'
>
> 'Sure you can.'
>
> 'You could also spin it.'
>
> 'Oh yes, that's called a rotation.'
>
> 'But that would be kinda hard for music, right?'
>
> 'Yup.'

The next step was to name the various transformations. Mathematicians have a number of terms at their disposal for describing the relationships among these figures. For example, the backwards cat might be called a reflection over the y-axis. It might also be called a vertical reflection, and in fact, this is the term we incorporated as Hardeep suggested the term when I was inviting the children to label the litter of cats. From there, we continued to label all of the other transformations, using combinations of various ideas until each child came up with a vocabulary of their own that others in the group could understand.

A week later, we moved to a musical manifestation of the same idea. I began by playing a motif of five notes on a small synthesiser, and then wrote the motif in the same position I had placed the first cat a week before. The children were able to generate all of the transformations of the motif, using the terms they had previously developed. Each of the transformations was played, and, as I had expected, some were met with approval while others were not.

I then introduced the pupils to the musical terms for each of the transformations – 'retrograde' for the backwards motif, 'inversion' for the upside-down motif, 'retrograde-inversion' for the upside-down and backwards motif, 'transposition' for the moved motif, and finally, 'diminution' and 'augmentation' for the faster and slower motifs, respectively. Thus, we had parallel language for the parallel transformations for each of the two disciplines (see Figure 5.6).

With more advanced pupils, I would also introduce algebraic expressions for each of the transformations, but this was both too difficult and unnecessary for the budding composers in Eileen's class. (See Upitis, 1990c, for a description of the transformations in algebraic terms.)

MATHS   MUSIC

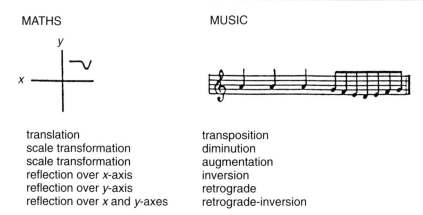

translation	transposition
scale transformation	diminution
scale transformation	augmentation
reflection over x-axis	inversion
reflection over y-axis	retrograde
reflection over x and y-axes	retrograde-inversion

Figure 5.6 Corresponding maths and music transformations

We were now ready to try our hand at composition through transformations. I gave each of the children a small piece of clear acetate with staff lines, and a few permanent overhead markers to share. I took a piece of this acetate myself, and demonstrated how they could use this simple technique to try all sorts of transformations of their motif. First, each child had to find five or six notes he or she liked, using their voices or one of the two small, inexpensive synthesiser keyboards that the children had brought from home. These notes were then written on the piece of acetate. Two of the children could read and write in standard musical notation, as could I, and we helped the others record their motifs on their pieces of acetate. Then the acetate pieces were flipped and moved, showing the transformations dealing with reflection and translation. These basic transformations were copied onto a piece of staff paper (see Figure 5.7). While we were doing this, Andrea kept glancing at the string art explorations of the Grade 4 pupils, and quietly noted: 'The Grade 4s are using symmetry too'.

Sometimes the transcriptions of the transformed motifs were not accurate. It was difficult for every child to record the notes from the acetate to the paper. As Eileen described previously, a similar thing happens when children first attempt to transcribe their geoboard figures on paper. When the children were transcribing a retrograde motif, for example, they would almost always get the right number of notes and the correct durations as well as the shapes for the new fragments, but they made mistakes in copying the precise musical intervals between the notes.

For example, if two notes were separated by a line and a space in the original, they might be separated only by a space when the child recorded the transformation. I pointed out the discrepancies to the group; however, I did not insist that each transformation be recorded accurately – it really did not matter one way or another. If the durations were accurate and the shape was correct, then the result was likely to be pleasing to the ear.

Figure 5.7 Creating basic music transformations with reflection

Once the children had recorded and labelled each of the transformations as accurately as they could, we had a discussion about how to pattern the melodic fragments they found appealing. There were numerous suggestions made about about how to generate a pattern. Many pupils pointed to patterns in the room, suggesting that a given colour could be attributed to a given melodic fragment and a composition could be assembled by following the patterns made by the colours. Someone suggested picking a tessellating pattern, and making a composition by following the tessellation.

I described how, some years back, a student had modelled her composition from the striped pattern on her sweater, using one colour for each of the melodic fragments. Another child suggested they could number each of the fragments they liked, and then generate a sequence using those numbers. This idea was pounced on by the others, and the children spent the rest of their time generating arithmetic and geometric sequences for use in patterning their music compositions.

Once the sequence was identified (I suggested limiting the sequence to 12 or 16 numbers, reflecting the conventions of Western music, where pieces are usually written in multiples of four or eight measures in length), the children wrote out their melodies following the sequence they had created. We played the melodies directly into a Macintosh computer, using a synthesiser and MIDI interface and the *Concertware* software. I played some of the melodies, and Andrea and Stephanie entered the others, as they were taking private piano lessons and had little difficulty reading the music.

All of us listened to each of the melodies from the printed scores. With pencils in hand, the composers marked areas they wanted to change, and the editing process began. Sometimes the changes were simple ones – like ending the piece on a lower note. Sometimes they were more complex – like repeating two bars, omitting one bar, and changing three or four notes in yet another bar (see Figure 5.8 for an example of edited and final work).

(a) Original motif and transformations

Figure 5.8 Moving from acetate transformations to the final form

In a few cases, the composer was so pleased with his or her composition, that the only change he or she wanted to make was to add a repeat sign – play it again, Sam.

I should add here that this project would have been very difficult to undertake without the availability of the computer as a tool for music composition. We relied on the computer (loaned to the classroom for the duration of this project) for the production of the notations, for the editing process (see Figure 5.9), and for the performance and recording of the polished compositions. This was not a case of using the computer because it was in the classroom – it was an example of finding a computer because the computer, synthesiser, and software were the best tools available for the project we had undertaken. Note also that the high technology of the computer was combined with the 'low' technology of clear acetate; just as with their tessellation explorations, pupils moved fluidly from one kind of tool or material to another.

(b) Computer notations and edits

(c) The final product

Figure 5.9 Editing music compositions

In the process of editing the compositions, many of the traditional rules of melody writing were expressed by the children. I remember well, as a beginning harmony student, hearing my teacher say, time and time again, 'Avoid large melodic leaps'. This was one of countless rules I was required to memorise. I often did not understand the reasons for the rules, and I rarely, if ever, discovered any of the rules for myself. While I began by memorising rules of harmony (Bill's compliance level), I later came to understand the rules (cognisance) and use them for composition (creation). Yet, in a few short hours, these children were articulating melody writing rules for themselves:

'That doesn't sound good because it's the only place it happens.'
[There is a convention or rule about using repetition.]

'I don't have it anywhere else, that's what's wrong.'
[Convention of repetition.]

'It doesn't sound good when it jumps like that.'
[Avoid large melodic leaps.]

'It goes too high there.'
[Avoid large melodic leaps.]

'It ends on the wrong note. It should end more down.'
[End on the tonic or home note.]

I added simple accompaniments to the melodies, based on the descriptions given by the children. Some asked for 'bouncy' accompaniments, others for 'marching', 'pretty', and 'boingy' ones. We simply did not have the time for each child to work out their own accompaniments. But this could have been done quite easily. I would have encouraged the children to use Orff xylophones and metallophones to work out their accompaniments, playing along with their melodies on the computer. These accompaniments could then have been added directly to the scores. Oh, to have the nine lives of a cat.

The pupils named their compositions and chose the instrument sound on the synthesiser they felt was best for performing their piece. Some chose conventional instruments, such as the horn or flute. Others incorporated 'spacier' sounds, such as 'ice-block' or 'stars'. At this point, one of the children suggested that they should write their own music for the animation soundtrack.

I taught them how to use the built-in sequencer on the synthesiser, and they began improvising compositions in small groups, with each person adding a new layer of sound until the composition was completed. A sequencer is like a series of tape recorders, where each 'track' is a different tape recorder. The sequencer allows the composer to record one track at a time, and then play the tracks simultaneously. The composer can listen to one track at a time, or any combination of the tracks. In our case, we had five tracks at our disposal. Different instruments could be used on each track, or the entire composition – all five tracks – could be played on the same instrument.

Using the sequencer as an improvisation tool went beyond composing music for the animation soundtrack. The children were also doing a unit on outer space at the time we were experimenting with composition, and one of them suggested they compose some music for their space projects. Although Hardeep pointed out there is no sound in space, someone retorted with: 'Well, we can imagine space music, can't we?', and so their imaginary space music project began.

I was delighted with the result, and pleased that they had suggested a meaningful way of integrating music into another curriculum unit. I was reminded, once again, of how skilled children are at making such connections – like Jaclyn seeing the symmetry of Bambi staring at his reflection in the pond.

Our work on music composition ended with a concert of compositions and yet another viewing of *The Changes*. Eileen and I watched the faces of the children as intently as they were watching the film and listening to their compositions. We watched their faces change from nervous anticipation to proud satisfaction as their work unfolded – a quiet drama spun without words or sound, but eloquent in its message; I wrote that, I made that, I am proud of that – I am an artist, a mathematician, an animator, a composer.

BILL

I will start this section with some reflections on the images of Eileen as a teacher as revealed in the first part of this chapter. I have never been in Eileen's classroom, and yet because of her fluency as a writer and my experience with a few other gifted teachers, I have constructed a strong sense of her ways of being with children. Rena, operating as an intermediary, has been able to confirm many of these intuitions. The prevailing image is that of a life of depth and richness, with strong interactions between the happenings in her classroom and the rest of her life.

The physical space is inviting and vibrant – the picture of Eileen struggling to find the few remaining patches of blackboard among posters of tessellating figures and Aboriginal art-work symbolises, for me, how far she has come from the traditional black-and-white, chalk-and-talk classroom. The materials are numerous and diverse, and resources are plentiful. Rena's description of helping Eileen move classrooms, two years after the research project ended, features tales of labelling and lugging forty large cartons filled with microscopes and maths manipulatives, rugs and pillows, balances and scales, wool and tiles, books and articles, rhythm instruments and audiotapes, pens and pencils, rulers and coloured markers, masks and magazines, and ribbons and string, down the stairs to the basement classroom she had requested because it had double the space of her old one. The extra room was needed, in part, because her old classroom did not adequately house four Macintosh

LC III computers and a printer which were now to be integrated into the classroom setting.

Those boxes held the string she used for her symmography activities described earlier in this chapter. Note again how the strong aesthetic connection with this topic and its associated motivating influence carries the children smoothly to concepts like negative numbers and co-ordinate systems, concepts which, with standard curricula and teaching approaches, would not be 'seen' by pupils for at least another four or five years. As noted previously, the educational value of materials is a function of the quality of ideas that emerge from their use. As is often the case, simple materials broadly used in the day-to-day lives of individuals can become the focus of wide ranging and profound mathematical research. We have seen this in the case of tiles, and it is also true in the case of string. The past decade has seen the emergence of knot theory which has connections with many branches of contemporary science (Adams, 1994).

Another aspect of Eileen's life which is shown in this chapter and is reflected in the experience of many fine teachers is the interplay between the roles of teacher and parent. It is not coincidental that some of the richest educational research on record originates with the observations made by scholars of their own children. One obvious example is the work of Jean Piaget, the genetic epistemologist whose entire theory of intellectual development was inspired by observations of his three children (Piaget, 1952; Gruber, 1977).

A contemporary and familiar educational movement – whole-language instruction – was significantly influenced in its early stages by Glenda Bissex's (1980) observations of her young son as he learned to read and write. A teacher reflecting on the activities of her own children at home is engaged in the same scholarly enterprise as Piaget and Bissex.

Incidents from the classroom can change perceptions at home, and family experiences can enrich classroom offerings. The roles of parent and teacher begin to merge; the satisfactions and challenges associated with one role become the generating images for the other. Having read these insights into her mathematical and other interactions with her young daughter Jaclyn, I was not surprised to find that Eileen had moved from her early and perhaps tentative beginnings in graduate study to the writing of an ambitious thesis on this very issue (Phillips, 1996).

Eileen has moved forward in another direction as well. I would now like to comment on the arrival of the four Macintosh computers that came *after* the year Rena spent with Eileen – the computers that, in part, necessitated the classroom change I described earlier. Like other elementary teachers, Eileen now has computers in her classroom, and she has heard many claims about the potential of this technology for enriching her curriculum. In fact, she has heard those claims from me, from Rena, from her thesis supervisor (Ann Anderson – the professor who originally introduced Rena and Eileen to one another), and from her more recent research colleague, Maria Klawe.

When Rena's time in Vancouver ended and she returned to Ontario, she left Eileen with a new possibility for continued research. One of Rena's sabbatical adventures was to become involved with E-GEMS, the large interdisciplinary research and development project directed by Dr Klawe, who was then head of the Computer Science department at UBC. Just as Ann had introduced Rena to Eileen, like a doublet chain, Rena had now introduced Maria to the wonders of Eileen's teaching and her classroom, and another series of research projects began.

Unlike the project work undertaken by Rena and Eileen reported here, however, the E-GEMS project put computer technology in the front and centre of classroom life. Eileen's use of computers now ranges from the increasingly common practice of using computers as writing and editing tools for words and graphics to the less common practice of field testing mathematical games as they are developed by the E-GEMS team. In the next section, I consider more ways in which information technology could now be of use to Eileen, and others like her who have computers in their classrooms on a permanent basis – computers that soon promise to be linked with one another and the rest of the planet through the Internet.

Technology and teaching – access to information through the Internet

The relatively small role played by computers in the activities described up to this point should not be interpreted as a reflection of any inherent incompatibility between the approaches used by Eileen and Rena and these tools. Indeed, under slightly different circumstances, the computer could become a very powerful component in this sort of learning environment, as it was for the composition project. The use of the computer as a composition tool would not have been possible even a few years ago.

In a similar way, the World Wide Web now has the potential to increase dramatically the research capabilities and the nature of contemporary mathematics and science for both teachers and pupils. I will illustrate this claim with reference to some of the ideas and projects described in previous chapters. I am aware that what follows will be easy to place in the all-too-common category of computer hype or Internet zealotry, perhaps partic-ularly by individuals who have had limited access to the sorts of tools described. One way of thinking about Internet access is as a form of distance rather than face-to-face education instead of emphasising the electronic aspect of computer connectivity.

The relationship of technology to human action and potential is complex, of long standing, and fraught with dangers (Dreyfus, Dreyfus and Athana-siou, 1986; Franklin, 1990; Postman, 1992; Weizenbaum, 1976). In particular, the history of classroom use of educational technology is filled with tales of grandiose claims followed by very modest impact (Cuban, 1986). There is no need to be as extreme as Negroponte (1995) to feel, nonetheless, that the various devices of information technology are going to have a very significant impact on many aspects of our lives (Turkle, 1984, 1995; Zuboff, 1988), not least in education.

It is clear that the engine, weaving looms, and the related machines of the industrial revolution altered physical work beyond recognition in the two centuries following 1760. That a parallel process involving the computer and its kindred devices is now well underway with respect to mental labour also seems undeniable. What remains to be seen is just how powerful this impact will ultimately be. Teachers, strategically placed to influence young minds, may well be one of the most potent forces shaping responses to these innovations (Papert, 1993).

The following examples should therefore be seen as nothing more than that. There is no inevitability about the role of computers in education; they are remarkably flexible tools, or perhaps more accurately, media – in the sense that they are also tools for making other tools. If, as seems likely, past trends continue, in some classrooms computers will be amplifiers for practices which are not in the best educational interests of children. Whereas in other classrooms, they will help to make already imaginative and effective practices even better. The potential is great. The challenge of realising it lies largely in the hands of individual teachers.

The Internet

To begin with, there is the field I mentioned in passing in Chapter 2, that of computational chemistry. This is, quite clearly, an unorthodox topic for an elementary school teacher to be investigating, but its very abstruseness can serve to make the point even more strongly. In the classical educational framework, access to a topic of this sort is quite difficult for non-specialists. Research reports have traditionally been published in specialised texts, journals and monographs which have been available only in the libraries of major corporations and universities.

This changed dramatically over a surprisingly short period of time. Now any person, anywhere in the world, provided they have access to the World Wide Web, can find within a matter of minutes, a great deal of up-to-the-minute information about this topic. A search for 'computational chemistry' by a major search engine (the Internet equivalent of a library card index) such as *Yahoo*, *InfoSeek*, *Open Text*, or *Alta Vista* will almost instantaneously locate resources available from research centres around the world.

Among these is a very readable report at the National Academy of Science Web Site in the form of an on-line publication entitled *Mathematical Challenges from Theoretical/Computational Chemistry*[10] and a site at New York University called MathMol[11] which includes among its objectives:

1) to provide students, teachers and the general public with information about the rapidly growing fields of molecular modelling and related areas, and, 2) to provide K-12 students with basic concepts in mathematics and their connection to molecular modelling.

Prominent in the materials which this project has generated to meet the second aim is an illustrated unit outlining an experiment to investigate the relative densities of water and ice. In the colourful pictures in this unit, I suspect that the children in Eileen's class would have had no difficulty recognising the fundamental issue at the heart of this question. This is because it is a relatively straightforward extension of their work on tessellations, the fitting of objects together on a flat surface in a patterned way. In the case of water and ice, the objects are molecules and the fitting has to be done in three dimensions.

From this note on the Internet there are many links to other sites which reveal glimpses of the power and beauty of contemporary mathematics and science. Among these are the pages on *Molecular Origami*,[12] and *Geometric Aspects of Protein Structure and Function*,[13] and *Quasicrystals*.[14]

The pictures on the quasicrystal page are exceptionally beautiful. Once again, there is a direct link from the work being carried out in some of the most advanced scientific laboratories in the world and the tessellation project of Eileen's pupils. This is because the theoretical basis for this exceptionally important area of scientific research comes from the mathematical play of the Oxford University mathematician Roger Penrose, of whom I wrote in Chapter 2, and his discovery of a new set of tiles which have come to be called after him, which tessellate, but which do not do so in a periodic way (Gardner, 1989).

One way to find out more about Penrose is, of course, to seek him out on the Web. Since he is a scholar who participates actively in many different areas of intellectual endeavour, a request for 'Penrose' on a powerful search engine will quickly reveal many possibilities for exploration (*Open Text* suggested 369 avenues to explore). The majority of these would be too specialised for general interest (the remarkable thing about Penrose is just how many different fields he contributes to – astrophysics, mathematics, computer science, psychology, and philosophy by no means exhaust the list), but one strong recommendation, as ranked by *Open Text* according to its criteria of 'best fit', is *The Penrose Puzzle Room*.[15]

This link takes us to an Internet-based business which specialises in art and puzzles based on the work of M. C. Escher. Because of Penrose's long-standing connection to Escher's work – Penrose and his father discovered the perpetual paradox which is the basis for the well-known Escher staircase and waterfall pieces – it makes sense to find a *Penrose Puzzle Room* as part of the *World of Escher* site. Several versions of puzzles derived from Penrose's non-periodic tiles are described. Also available from this site is a demonstration (the saving and printing options have been disabled) version of the software *Tesselmania!* which I commented on earlier.

Easy access to the World Wide Web is still relatively rare in teaching circles. This is, however, changing rapidly. For teachers who do have access to this tool, the availability of the demonstration version of *Tesselmania!* is a good example of the way in which access to many educational materials is likely to be handled in the future. In the past, it was often frustrating to read about new materials in journals or to hear about them at conferences and to have no way to try them out.

The early days of Logo are a case in point – papers, presentations, and rumours leaked out of MIT and a few other hardware-intensive universities for years before a public version of the language became available, not coincidentally, with the arrival of personal computers in the early 1980s. And yes, the Internet has changed that considerably as well. A very robust and potent version of Logo is available as freeware from Brian Harvey's homepage at Berkeley.[16]

And now, one final connection from the *World of Escher* site to our book. The excellent book by Seymour and Britton (1989) *Introduction to Tessellations* concludes with an invitation (on the two pages following p. 256) to students to participate in the second 'Escher-Like Art Contest'. When Rena told the Grade 3s about this possibility they expressed interest in participating. It seems likely then that they would also have found the tessellation contest run from the *World of Escher* to be something of which they would like to be part.

The educational differences between the book and Internet versions of the tessellation contest are worth noting. The book is fixed in time in a way the computer is not. In this book, originally published in 1989 and in its fourth printing in 1991, the entry deadline for the contest is given as June 30, 1992. After that time there is no easy way to know whether or not the contest is still being run. It certainly does not make sense to spend another £15 for a reprinted version of the book which may differ from the first only in the date of the contest.

With the Internet version, updating of information is much easier as is communication, via e-mail, with the contest organisers. In addition, it is possible to see some of the pieces which have been submitted to the contest. In the current entries file,[17] as this section is being written, three very different submissions were viewable. The two entries with university addresses, *Maozou* and *Penrose stairs*, which presumably would be judged in the '18-and-over, computer-generated' category, were technically very accomplished, but for my taste, the mixtures of colours and light, like a cathedral window, in Katie Murphy's *Alphabet Soup* (Adams Elementary School, Omaha, NE, USA) made it the 'best of the class'. The price paid for this easy accessibility is increased ephemerality. Because Web pages are often generated and supported only by individuals, it is easy for the pages to vanish into cyberspace. (I wonder if Katie Murphy's *Alphabet Soup* is still available.)

Another general fear about the use of information technology is that it may tend to be a 'dehumanising' force in coming years. This is not a worry which can be dismissed out of hand as the partners of many Internet surfers can testify: 'get a modem – lose a life' is a catch phrase that resonates deeply in many high-tech circles. There is a sense, however, in which some aspects of Internet use can be seen as increasing our commitment to human values and activity. One example of this is the way in which easy information access can permit us to have a feeling of 'knowing' another individual in some non-trivial ways even though we have never had face-to-face contact. To a certain extent, this is true in the previously cited case of Roger Penrose. At least two Penrose Web pages include a photograph and one of them goes into some detail about his background and interests.

The case of another scientist, Donald Knuth, whose work I mentioned earlier, pushes this point further. It is likely that many readers will not have heard previously of Dr. Knuth. Prior to the advent of networked personal computers, an expedition to find out anything significant about this prominent computer scientist would have required a visit to a fairly large library. With the advent of the Web, the space between interest and query can be almost non-existent. Putting *Open Text*[18] (my current favourite engine, as previous examples have revealed) on the trail of 'Knuth Stanford' generates 430 possibilities including an extended interview with Computer Literacy Bookshops, Inc.[19] In this eight-page exchange, which also includes a picture – the image is that of a relaxed, warm and somewhat rumpled man – Knuth gives a number of quite fascinating insights into the life of the individual who is 'considered by many to be the world's pre-eminent computer scientist' (p. 1 of the interview).

Having read the interview, I came away with a sense that I have a much better feel for the field of computer science, the sorts of working habits and life choices made by a first-class researcher, and insights into the thoughts of a formidable mind. The contrast with the vision of the discipline and its practitioners that I get from most textbooks is great. Among these insights are his ideas about exciting areas for new thinkers to work in: 'Biology easily has 500 years of exciting problems to work on' (he is less certain about computer science); and the fact that he no longer uses electronic mail – for the issues that are important to him the disadvantages outweigh the advantages. He explains it this way:

> E-mail is wonderful for some people, absolutely necessary for their job, and they can do their work better. I like to say that for people whose role is to be on top of things, electronic mail is great. But my role is to be on the bottom of things. I look at ideas and think about them carefully and try to write them up.... I move slowly through things that people have done and try to organise the material. But I don't know what is happening this month.

His conception of what is important in his professional career is interesting – *The Art of Computer Programming* was a project that he began work on some thirty years ago. In his preliminary outline he had seven chapters. It was after Chapter 1 hit 700 pages that he realised that he had a problem on his hands! The first three 'chapters' all became famous texts in their own right (Knuth, 1968, 1969, 1973).

In commenting on why he had decided to retire early, he notes:

> I realised that my main goal in life was to finish *The Art of Computer Programming*; I had looked ahead and seen that it would take twenty years of work, full-time. If I continued doing everything else that I was doing, it was going to be forty or fifty years of work. I was just not getting anywhere, I was getting further and further behind. So I said, 'Enough'.

In commenting on his personal interests, Knuth has the following interchange with the interviewer.

CLB: You have many interests outside of computing and mathematics – music, religion, writing. Is music a creative outlet for you, a means of recreation, or a spiritual outlet?

Knuth: At the moment it's recreational. I like to have friends come to the house and play four-hands piano music. If I could do it every week, I would. I hope to live long enough so that after I've finished my life's work on *The Art of Computer Programming*, I might compose some music. Just a dream. . . . It might be lousy music, of course.

And, of possible interest in a book on this theme:

CLB: Any changes in the quality of the students [referring to students at Stanford University]?

Knuth: Not the quality … but they don't know as much about mathematics as they used to.

A direct search for the word 'doublets' reveals a dazzling choice from non-overlapping fields as unalike as theoretical physics ('A nucleus with octupole deformation of the mean field reveals rotational doublets with the same angular momentum and opposite parity. Mediated by the Coriolis-type interaction, the doublet structure leads to a strong regular component in the parity violation caused by weak interaction'), religion and politics ('these doublets actually contradict one another' in *Corruption of the Torah*), backgammon ('Doublets if the same number appears on both dice') and literature ('nobles, in doublets of crimson velvet' – from Mark Twain's *The Prince and the Pauper*). Unfortunately, none of these uses has anything in common with our meaning of the term, so in this case the Internet might seem to have struck out.

A little (well, actually, a lot) of random surfing would, however, reveal a very active 'word ladder' list run by the publishers at MathPro.[20] They pose 'word ladder' challenges, which they describe as follows.

For your enjoyment, a word ladder puzzle is published daily at the Puzzle Junction.

DIRECTIONS: Transform the initial word to the target word by a sequence of intermediate words. Each word is obtained from the previous one by changing exactly one letter.

For example: 'ROUND' can be changed to 'COUNT' in 3 steps by the sequence:

ROUND – MOUND – MOUNT – COUNT.

And finally to return to the topic with which Eileen started this chapter, kaleidoscopes. A direct search would reveal a page run by Brett Bensley,[21] devoted to this theme which includes a section on how to make a kaleidoscope. A slightly more extensive search would reveal a unit in the materials available from the Franklin Institute[22] called *Film Canister Kaleidoscope* which starts as follows:

> Grade Level: 4–6 Discussion:
> In this project, the children are exposed to symmetry in the familiar form of a kaleidoscope. As an extra bonus, this project recycles materials which otherwise might be thrown away.

Having argued at some length that the Internet can be seen as a powerful, emerging tool for teachers, it is important to keep its use in perspective. As I have noted with respect to Donald Knuth, there are times when even those of us who see it in a positive light can be overwhelmed. In a recent paper, subtitled *Not for Everyone, Not for Everything*, Rena put it this way:

> I am concerned that people not using technology will feel 'left out' or 'behind the times'. As one of my students once remarked, 'I'm worried about all of this hypertext business. I'd be lucky to get to slightly agitated text!' (Perhaps, more aptly put, the real concern is the danger of having some people feel inept or inadequate in the face of new technology.) I am equally concerned that some who make liberal use of technology will want to use technology for certain things that are better accomplished with much older forms of non-computer-driven technology (like pen and paper).
>
> (Upitis, 1995b)[23]

In that spirit, it is perhaps appropriate to end this section with the observation that despite all the intriguing material related to this general topic of kaleidoscopes that one might reel in from the Web, by far the best set of resources, in my opinion, would be the marvellous, not-new, but nevertheless highly imaginative and mathematically rich set of 'mirror books', by Marion Walter, *Annette* (1971), *Another, Another, Another and More* (1975) and *The Mirror Puzzle Book* (1985). As we explore the Internet in the years to come, we would do well to remind ourselves to search the shelves of second-hand bookshops as well.

Chapter 6

Children as mathematicians
'I discoverded it'

RENA: researcher, teacher and mathematician

Despite some recent and well-directed qualifying statements, an over-whelming number of elementary school teachers in North America have embraced a 'whole-language' approach to the teaching of reading and writing over the past couple of decades. With this approach, children are encouraged to develop their own forms of communicating through speech and text, while immersed in an environment rich in the literature of many genres. The whole-language classroom is a lively one – children write, read, converse, and write some more. By being actively engaged in reading and writing, children become writers and critics of literature.[24]

The sweep of the whole-language movement has been nothing short of remarkable, but other disciplines have been slow to follow suit. I would argue that mathematics is only half-way there. Many teachers have moved towards more frequent use of manipulative materials in mathematics. Rather than relying solely on mathematical workbooks and textbooks, teachers use brightly-coloured manipulative materials, like pattern blocks and geoboards, to help pupils explore aspects of geometry. Common objects, such as lolly sticks, are also called on to help children learn about place value.

By using concrete objects and recording their findings, children are not only more likely to remember what they have been taught, but indeed, they are more likely to discover for themselves certain concepts that were previously presented solely by the classroom teacher.[25]

However, unlike the whole-language movement in which children are creating their own poetry and prose, changes in mathematics teaching have not yet reached this next stage. At the moment, manipulative materials are used primarily to *learn about* mathematics, rather than to *make* mathematics. While teachers may encourage their pupils to discover which shapes tessellate through the use of pattern blocks, it takes a qualitative change in orientation to draw on the understanding of concepts in order to *create* something with that understanding. (Incidentally, as one of the children pointed out, most pattern blocks tessellate, so it is difficult to learn about the special cases like pentagons; see Chapter 2.)

In asking children to work at making silk paintings, animated films, paper jewellery, kaleidoscopes and music compositions, Eileen and I have tried to help pupils not only learn maths in a compliant way, but also to understand it (cognisance), and to be able to use it (creation of artifacts as well as mathematical discovery). In this work, we have been guided by a theoretical orientation that embraces the view that learning occurs through social interaction, and that knowledge is constructed through social interaction.[26] Such knowledge can be evidenced in a number of ways: in this book, we have explored examples of knowledge-making through creative products.

The other projects

There are two kinds of projects not described in the previous chapters – the abandoned projects and the projects yet to be – akin to Scrooge's Ghosts of Christmas Past and Future. The past ghosts – projects that, for one reason or another, simply never made it off the ground; the future ghosts – the projects yet to be – those great ideas that Eileen and I had as the year went on, but could not incorporate into our plans. While this book is a description of the Ghosts of Christmas Present, the story is incomplete without the other two. Unlike Scrooge, however, I am willing to look Past and Future Ghosts straight in the eye. I will start with Christmas Past.

Some of the great ideas we had for the children turned out not to be so great – at least not this year, not with these children, and not in the way that we introduced them. Rather than leaving the impression that everything we touched turned into curriculum gold, it is important to acknowledge some of the ideas that, for one reason or another, just did not take off. And in some cases, the 'great ideas' simply could not be realised because of the constraints of the school year – we ran out of time.

Work on codes was one of the abandoned projects. Bill and I have long been interested in symbols and notations, and a project on codes seemed a good idea. This project began as did all the others; I offered some ideas to introduce the topic, and I intended to let the specific focus evolve out of the interests of the children.

I started with various codes to decipher, including a hexagon 'codex' that the children could use to decipher my message as well as writing messages of their own (see Figure 6.1). This worked well as an introductory activity; the children quickly found ways to become efficient in their decoding, and took delight in finding short-cuts.

Doug proudly announced: 'The "e" is always on ten! I'm going to do all the tens.' They took the next part of the activity (writing their own coded sentences) seriously. Tanya announced: 'I'm going to make a *true* sentence', and spent some time deciding on the precise words to use.

The children encountered two difficulties in making their own sentences with the codex, and found various ways of solving them both. The first was dealing with numbers. Jon asked: 'What if you need a number in your sentence? Can you use Roman numerals?' Another answered: 'You could just use normal numbers – or make up a number code!'

The second challenge involved spacing between words. Erika was one of the first to finish, and passed her coded sentence to Stephanie for deciphering. Stephanie ran the first two words together, and became confused. Erika then placed an asterisk at the end of each word, and Stephanie read her message easily. Having witnessed the interchange between Stephanie and

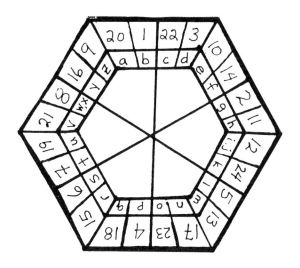

22–20–17   16–23–19   14–12–17–3

7–11–10   22–23–3–10 ?   17–23–8

13–20–24–10   23–17–10   23–14

16–23–19–15   23–8–17.

Figure 6.1 A hexagon 'codex'

Erika, Hardeep invented his own system to separate words: 'Those lines in between mean they're new words.' Others used spaces, as I had done in the original message.

This was evidently an enjoyable session – no less so than the first session for tessellations or composition, for example. At the end, enthusiasm was high:

'I *love* this. Can we do it next time?'

'Oh oh. School's over. I have to go back to my desk. Oh boy. I don't believe it.'

'Luckily I came this afternoon. I was sick this morning.'

I began the next session with a general discussion of codes, and one of the children mentioned postal codes as an example. The children became enthusiastic about deciphering the Canadian Postal Code system, and for several sessions, gathered data from various sources for this purpose. After exhausting their own postal codes and marking them on the Vancouver map, some of the children roamed the various corners of the school looking for new codes from library staff, other teachers, the custodian, and so on.

Initially, they were convinced the 'V' in the postal code stood for Vancouver ('Postal code! Mine's V6N 2K2. V for Vancouver, right?'), although it actually stands for the province of British Columbia. When they found someone who lived in New Westminster (another adjoining town) with a postal code also beginning with 'V', they were convinced that the 'V' must stand for something else, and eventually worked out the solution. Over the next couple of days, many of the children came in with long collections of postal codes and corresponding addresses of friends and relatives all over the country. Rishma brought in posters she had made of Persian numbers and the alphabet – a code is a code (see Figure 6.2).

So what went wrong? There was plenty of engagement at the outset, and children were making links between the codes we were examining in class and codes in other contexts. My sense is that three things conspired against us. The first was simply the rhythm of the school year; we started this work just before the Christmas holidays, and when the children returned from the break, they were ready for something new. We were not deeply enough involved in this work to pick up from where we had left off.

The second factor was the attraction of something more compelling – somehow making an animated film (see Chapter 3) had more appeal than deciphering the Canadian Postal Code system. (As Jon said: 'You can just look it up in the post office. They have all the books there.') And finally, we had not developed a project from this work – all of the other explorations (e.g., tessellations, animation, symmetry) had a product associated with them – a silk painting, a film, a kaleidoscope, or whatever. No such product had yet been associated with codes.

Figure 6.2 Rishma's Persian alphabet

While I might have come up with something (maybe something to do with secret codes and treasure hunts), it made no sense to do this simply to prolong a project that was naturally coming to a close. This does not mean that the work we did was not worthwhile nor that a study of codes is not 'real' mathematics; it simply means that there are times, in the life of the classroom, when some things need to be put aside. It may also be that Bill would have been the natural person to bring this work forward, given his love for puzzles.

And what of Ghosts of the Christmas Future? These were projects that Eileen and I thought of, but were not able to bring to fruition during the school year – projects for another time. Early in January, Eileen showed me a beautiful book she had bought on fractals. Fractals form a relatively new area of mathematics dealing with the 'mysterious order in chaos' – including various patterned but non-linear natural phenomena like ocean shorelines, ferns, and snowflakes (Briggs, 1992, p. 13; see Figure 6.3). A more formal definition might say something about finite area and infinite perimeter, but I prefer to think of the world of fractals in terms of the ferns I see when I am walking through the woods.

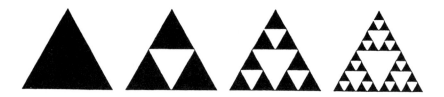

Figure 6.3 The Sierpinski gasket – a simple fractal

Eileen bought the fractals book both for its gorgeous illustrations and because she wanted to be able to attach more meaning to the frequently heard term 'fractal'. I had previously learned something of fractals in some work I did with Logo in the early 1980s, and in discussions with colleagues about shorelines. But how could fractals be used as the basis for a creative mathematical project for eight-year-olds? Logo was not an easy option in this particular setting, and I wanted to work, as much as possible, in the circumstances as I found them. Could we make fractals without sophisticated technology, computer or otherwise?

Quite by chance, a possibility presented itself. I had been experimenting with different ways of painting oceanscapes in watercolours. One cold night – the temperature was below zero – I painted outdoors, hoping that some of the paint would freeze into unexpected and ocean-like shapes. To my surprise, some beautiful ice crystals formed and remained on the paper. Fractals! Then began the weeks of waiting for the right temperature (the perfect conditions I had on the first night were the result of good luck rather than good planning) and judging the accuracy of the weather forecast so I would know whether to bother setting my alarm for this night-time adventure.

When it was cold enough (about –3 °C), I would venture out in the wee hours of the morning, and, armed with my paints, wet paper, and headlamp, paint away on the back patio. (Only a few neighbours saw me, and they already thought I was eccentric, so no harm done.) The world of fractals opened before my very eyes. (Having learned more about water and ice from Bill's Internet reference in the previous chapter, I can now imagine endless ways of exploring mathematics with water and colour, warmth and cold. Bring on the winter.)

But fractals remained a Ghost of Christmas Future for room 108; I made my discovery at the very end of the winter, and it simply was not cold enough during the day to make ice fractal paintings. (Eileen and I briefly conspired to arrange a midnight field trip to the school parking lot, but abandoned that notion soon enough.)

By the time we were half-way into tessellations, Eileen and I were generating more ideas for maths projects than we would ever have imagined possible. By seeing the world through a mathematical lens, everything began to look like mathematics. With more time, we would have made quilts, paper, more music, batik, planted gardens, sewn giant pillows in the shape of fruit slices and wedges, made clay pots and built pits to fire them in, and mapped out trails in the woods. And, having learned from our conversations with Bill, we would have explored Carroll's doublets, Knuth's theory, and a range of other ideas from the Internet. Another time.

I have one more story to tell from our year together, before I close.

Of children, impostors and mathematicians

In the spring of the year I spent in Eileen's classroom, I took a trip to Boston for a couple of days. The reason for the trip was to meet with researchers, mathematicians, educators, and computer scientists about a new project involving electronic games. Part of our visit included a meeting at MIT – the Massachusetts Institute of Technology.

Late in the afternoon, standing in the hallway, I found myself wedged between two remarkable professors, both of them colleagues and friends of mine. Each had two doctoral degrees, in mathematics and in theoretical computer science. In passing, I made a comment about concave quadrilaterals, and the fact that even they tessellate (see Figure 6.4). My statement was challenged. I held my ground for a few minutes, telling them about the hundreds of tiles and pieces of cardboard I had manipulated that year with a group of eight-year-olds. I told them how we had cut out every kind of quadrilateral we could think of, and placed them on the floor with 'no floor showing'. I thought to myself that the concave quadrilateral was the *Star*

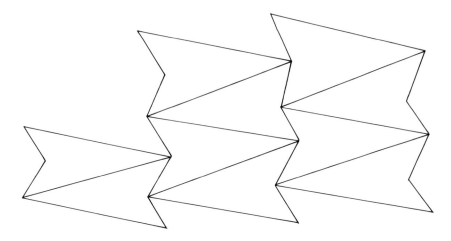

Figure 6.4 Tessellating concave quadrilaterals

Fleet Command symbol of the *Star Trek* movie and television series that Hardeep had used in his silk card tessellation. And I thought about how, when cutting concave quadrilaterals out of sandpaper to make paper jewellery, I hardly ever had any scraps left over.

Both of these professors, in different ways, argued I was wrong. They claimed this was one class of quadrilaterals that simply would not tessellate. One of them offered me a proof, which I refused to entertain. The other offered me a counter-example, which was more compelling to me, and I examined it closely. Both of them spoke with the authority of degrees and years of being professional mathematicians. More people started to crowd around us, and offered more counter-examples and extreme cases. I was convinced by their arguments.

Nonetheless, on the trip home, I took out a pair of scissors and a piece of paper, and littered the aeroplane with more quadrilaterals. If I were wrong, I had to demonstrate this fact to myself by the methods I knew best. To my surprise, after a while I found I could make any particular concave quadrilateral tessellate.

The next morning I took a walk. It was April in Vancouver, and raining. I thought about that concave quadrilateral once again, and about things like 360 degrees in a complete rotation. I thought about the four corners of a quadrilateral – the bulb, the soil, the sun, and the rain. And I wondered if, as long as those four existed together, the flower would grow – and the quadrilateral would tessellate.

Later in the day, I worked out a kind of a proof (in my own notation – not a formal proof, as I am still not facile in standard mathematical notations and conventions). Then I looked up the 'Case of the Concave Quadrilateral' (this had reached mystery proportions for me) in a book (yes, another kind of authority). Sure enough, there I found a formal proof for the claim that all quadrilaterals tessellate, using numbers and letters instead of soil and bulbs.

But of course the lesson for me had nothing to do with 'the right answer'. Rather, this was a lesson about how my own belief and trust in my evidence was shaken by authority. It was about having to work out a solution – *slowly* – in a way that made sense to me. It was about me being a mathematician, perhaps in the same way that a child can be a mathematician. It was about puzzling through. It was about individual differences and learning styles. It was about confidence in my own ways of knowing.

I admitted in the first chapter that I feel that I am something of an impostor in the field of mathematics – that I am approaching mathematics through the back door. My way of understanding mathematics is to make sense of it through music, through language, and through the patterns I understand as a potter and a painter. I have come to realise that my way of being a mathematician, like that of the children I encountered in Eileen's class, is perhaps dependent upon an intuitive first encounter, but nonetheless it is a way of making sense of mathematics – different, perhaps, from formal systems, but importantly grounded in experience and creation. Perhaps I am not an impostor after all.

EILEEN: teacher, researcher and mathematician

What would 'whole mathematics' look like if it were fully implemented? If it were modelled on whole language, it would consist of pupils being mathematicians. But what exactly defines a mathematician? When I have asked this question to children and adults alike, I routinely get answers that include:

- someone who is good at maths;
- someone who works with numbers;
- someone who likes to solve problems;
- a genius or a brain;
- like an accountant or a banker;
- a person who sees maths in everything;
- a person who studies patterns of numbers;
- a person who teaches maths at university;
- not a person who does just computations;
- a person who forms hypotheses and works on answers using numbers;
- a very logical, ordered person;
- a person who uses creative strategies to solve logic problems.

When I ask myself the same question, I feel, more than I know, the answer. My belief is that a mathematician is someone with a special way of viewing his or her world – a person who sees and can talk about patterns and connections, in both living and non-living entities. A mathematician has the ability to stop and enjoy mathematical beauty. A mathematician is someone who can generalise from specifics and who can generate specifics from generalisations. A mathematician can often create a multitude of strategies to solve a problem. Even when a problem has only one 'right' answer, a mathematician can construct several possible routes to get to the answer. Hence, professional life is an open-ended adventure for a mathematician.

This view is quite different from the one I once held. As a high-school student, I vividly recall thinking and feeling that mathematicians were cold, closed-minded, extremely rational people. Following logic and blind obedience to rules seemed the only way to attain entry into the world of a mathematician. At that time, as I described in the first chapter, it appeared to me that the world of a mathematician must be dull, joyless, and extremely predictable. Yet, somehow, I always felt it should be more. Even then, I could see room for expansion.

After many years spent teaching all subjects and a range of grades from Kindergarten to Grade 7, I finally feel that I am on the edge of some discoveries about the direction this expansion could take. I believe pupils need support in developing their intuitions and their informal mathematical abilities. I believe in valuing the sense-making aspects of mathematics that our pupils possess when they enter school.

As an example of this here is another anecdote about my younger daughter, Jaclyn. At three-and-a-half years old, she and I were sitting at a table sharing a bag of cheese puffs.

Mum: Here, I'll dump some out.
Jaclyn: That's a lot. Let's count. 1, 2, 3, 4, 5, 6, 7, 8, 9, 10, 11, 12, 13, 18.
Mum: 14! Wow, that is a lot!
Jaclyn: You can have some.
Mum: Let's share like this. One for you, one for me, one for you, one for me [Jaclyn takes over until the pile is divided].
Mum: We each have seven.
Jaclyn: Are we the same? (She pairs them up, end-to-end)

Mum: Yes.

Mum: Now, look at this. [I spread mine out as indicated in (b) below.] Do
I have more, or do we both have the same?

Jaclyn: Let's see. [She moves her puffs to align with mine.] The same.

In Piaget's conservation experiments, young children typically say that a line
of items contains more when it is spread out. This situation came to mind as
Jaclyn and I were discussing how many cheese puffs we each had, and I could
not resist a 'natural' opportunity to try it. Jaclyn reacted to my question with
a problem-solving attitude, rather than seeing what she said as a single-
answer response (guess). She chose to use pairing as her strategy, perhaps
because she had just used it to determine if our piles of puffs had the same
number in them.

The important thing for me is that she felt free to manipulate the objects
in order to come up with her answer, and that she did this manipulation prior
to responding. This suggests to me that she was uncertain about the answer
and needed to construct a solution. This also suggests that she was using
maths to make sense of my question and the visual information she needed
in order to interpret it. Based on many observations such as this single one,
I believe most children come to school with a mathematical attitude that
encourages them to use mathematics as a sense-making tool. (For more on
this issue, see Phillips and Anderson, 1993.) Sense-making, as we have shown,
can occur as a consequence of creating artifacts; though, of course, in more
conventional classwork, I also supported pupils as they worked on sense-
making through the discovery and exploration of mathematical ideas
directly.

In addition to recognising and valuing pupils' early mathematical experiences, we need to expand our pupils' general mathematical backgrounds. By
this, I mean their awareness of famous mathematicians (including women),
and their recognition and acknowledgement of an assortment of mathematical tools.

Without doubt, my pupils received a very broad education in mathematics. Yet, nevertheless, when I asked them, on a written survey at the end
of the year, to name some famous mathematicians, many of them could not
come up with one individual other than 'Miss Upitis' or 'Ms Phillips'.
However, when asked to name some famous authors, musicians, and artists,
most of the pupils could come up with more than one individual for each of

these categories. This let me know that I need to add this human face of mathematics to my curriculum. This is one more stage in making mathematics real – associating mathematics with people.

When I ask my pupils to write a list of tools that mathematicians use, I usually receive responses like 'calculators, computers, scales, rulers, and paper and pencil'. During the year of these maths projects, some pupils also responded with answers like 'a piece of string, a pile of pebbles, tangrams, pattern blocks, and pieces of tile'. For me, it indicated a shift away from computation as the only form of mathematics that children can identify.

When asked what they, as children, do that is like the work of a mathematician, usually the first response involves description of an arithmetic operation like adding, subtracting, multiplying or dividing. A few terms like fractions, geometry, decimals, and measurement are also often given. During the year of these projects, many wrote that they solved problems, while others mentioned that they estimated, and others again said that they talked together.

When I discussed their responses with the class, the pupils' answers expanded and became increasingly imaginative. It was as if they were feeding off one another, one response seeding another. Oral discussion opened their minds to the mathematics around them, or perhaps, reminded them of the mathematics they had already used. Throughout the year, these pupils had been extremely verbal and adventurous in their explorations about mathematics, not only in our projects but also in their 'regular' maths as well. Yet, in responding independently to a written survey, not all of what I saw as mathematical was mentioned: it took the familiar, discursive situation to gain access to their connections.

More than anything else, this confirmed my belief in the crucial role that discussion can play in sense-making in mathematics. Talking about these activities provided the integrating factor needed to connect the world beyond school to their work on mathematics projects within school. Talking also provided the link between mathematical projects and more traditional forms of school mathematics. Such talking is a powerful tool to broaden the scope of mathematics for pupils.

In summary, how can the scope of school mathematics for pupils be broadened? First, we must enrich the definition for ourselves, and then we must employ some of the things we know from learning theory and from the 'whole-language' approach to enrich our mathematics classes. Whole mathematics could have a universal goal of encouraging children to 'do mathematics like a mathematician', in the same way that whole language has pupils reading like authors and writing like writers.

How might we see mathematicians as great questioners, and encourage pupils to become question askers? How might we see mathematicians as people who apply mathematics to solve problems, and encourage pupils to solve problems and undertake projects in mathematics? How might we see mathematicians as people who are skilled in seeing things in a variety of ways, and encourage pupils to be divergent thinkers who can formulate multiple solution paths? How might we encourage open communication amongst pupil mathematicians, and foster attitudes of persistence and self-confidence?

The pupils involved in the maths projects in room 108 certainly asked questions, solved problems, created models, wrote and talked about mathematics. Their communication took various and sometimes unexpected forms. For example, Darren completed a report on pioneer days, and involved comparisons between the way maths used to be taught (mostly by rote) and the way he experienced it nowadays. He wrote: 'A long time ago at school they did math[s] a different way. They would memorise their math[s] problems. Nowadays, we do a lot more thinking [than] they used to.'

As Bill has indicated, we could have emphasised the art or developed the language arts factors involved in the projects, but we chose to attend to the mathematics. I do not think much of the mathematics would have been readily available to most of the children without adult mediation. The pupils needed to be prompted to reflect on the maths involved in creating a piece of jewellery, a weaving, a tessellation, a silk card, a piece of string art, a music composition, an animated film, or a kaleidoscope, much as they needed to be prompted at the end of the year when Rena and I discussed their responses to the maths survey.

I have been carried away with the 'teachable moment' many times in the past, only to realise that an activity was being pursued without the initial groundwork being firmly in place. At the very least, the children need a mental framework upon which to hook their new learning.

Rena has claimed that manipulative materials are used primarily to learn about mathematics, rather than to make mathematics. In encouraging pupils to be mathematicians, teachers are responsible for providing them with the opportunity to use manipulatives as tools. These tools can help the pupil find answers (learn about mathematics), and can also help the pupil construct mathematics, both conceptually and strategically.

The use of manipulatives needs to be mediated, or they may fall into the category of 'crutches' and their use will be scorned by those teachers who feel that they should not create 'dependencies' on the part of their pupils. Also, without mediation, the connection between the tool and the maths may not be clearly established. For me, the power of manipulative materials lies in the child's interpretation of their use and the child's conceptual construction based on their use. I have seen manipulatives be mathematically empowering. My pupils feel that using manipulatives is 'harder than just doing the question with paper and pencil' and that 'manipulatives really make you think'.

I agree with Rena that pupils have to *make* objects with mathematics if they are to experience themselves as mathematicians. But, like Bill, I would include activities like games in my list of ways to 'make' mathematics. Part of the making of mathematics involves sense-making which I discussed earlier; another draws on the application of these concepts to real-world situations and real-world problems. These thoughts bring me to one of the main questions raised by the accounts in this book: how have pupils become better mathematicians by being involved with these projects?

First, pupils actively had to *use* mathematical ideas to complete these projects. They needed to take such concepts and apply them. Pupils with less experience or fewer opportunities to create the initial mathematical constructions produced less desirable finished pieces. Cognition and process produced better results than imitation.

Pupils also needed the skills to communicate mathematically. They needed to be able to ask questions, give examples, demonstrate, and explain. Pupils learned to collaborate and co-operate with each other during both the lead-up to the projects and the carrying out of them. Children wrote about and discussed their projects with each other and with us. They enjoyed the opportunity to communicate with someone else involved in the project, and did not feel threatened, as children sometimes do, when asked to explain what they were working on.

Some of the mathematical attitudes I saw developing in my pupils, more than I have noticed in other years, included the following:

• they were persistent, willing to take chances and encouraging of the strategies of others;
• they did not mind if something did not work the first time; they were happy to try again;
• they developed in self-confidence.

When Rena talked about her self-doubts in the face of mathematical authorities (concave quadrilaterals at MIT), I found myself thinking that this probably would not have happened to most of the children involved in this project. They would not have paused to give respectful doubt a chance. Their response would have immediately been: 'I know it can be done. I'll prove it.' They have developed confidence in their own ways of representing mathematical knowledge.

When teachers teach thematically, I often find the mathematics component is relegated to number facts on cut-out shapes that fit the theme. Adding two-digit numbers on a sheet shaped like a bear is not maths integration (see Bill's discussion in an earlier chapter about integration, where he gives the example of adding sums on orange, pumpkin-shaped paper being neither good mathematics nor good art, and also Jardine, 1995): neither is completing spelling assignments on pumpkin-shaped paper language integration. The integration of maths into a theme is often forced and phoney, mainly because maths facts and computations are not at the heart, either of the theme, or of mathematics. Rather than trying to force the integration of maths into something, it is time for teachers to integrate other areas into maths. Maths projects like the ones we have described are one way of integrating subjects in a more authentic way.

In general, the structure for our maths project development was:

- maths concepts (or situations and materials rich with possibility) are presented and each pupil is allowed time to construct his or her own way of representing knowledge and to express that knowledge through discussion;
- standard algorithms are taught through sense-making models and representations;
- pupils are given ample opportunity for self-construction of the process and for discussion with others;
- finally, projects are undertaken that build upon the pupils' knowledge of concepts and processes – this feeds back into a deeper understanding of the original ideas presented.

Maths projects provided the link between 'school maths' and 'real-world maths'. They acted as an empowering agent, as witnessed in Doug's 'I discoverded it'. Pupils need all the positive, confidence building, sense-making activities we can provide: without these, maths returns to the land of rote-learning and memorising. This is a very shaky foundation upon which to build mathematical understanding.

I recently watched a 'formerly-solid' student in mathematics become completely deflated and almost destroyed mathematically when memorised knowledge stopped making sense. We speak of 'solid' pupils in a positive way; now it provides me with a different image – an image of bricks or structures, and rigid rules, falling. Perhaps we should not be developing 'solid' pupils – maybe 'flexible' would better describe the 'good' maths pupils.

As this teenager's support structures toppled, so did her self-confidence – self-confidence she needed to face her mathematical shambles. She felt dumb and confused. How could this happen to a good pupil, one who was allowed to enrol in 'enriched' maths classes? I believe it was because her maths knowledge was based on rules and not on self-constructions. When maths started to get a little more complicated than her memory alone could handle, she had nothing to fall back on. She had learned *about* doing mathematics, but she had never really *made mathematics* for herself, at least not in school. Maths was devoid of real purpose and meaning. The enriched maths she experienced was nothing more than advanced computation – 'Give them more and let's make it harder'.

Through the use of manipulative materials and beyond – into maths projects – I hope to prevent such a collapse from happening to my pupils. I want them to develop greater mathematical power that will keep them interested in maths, not only as a subject, but as a way of viewing the world. I hope they will develop themselves as mathematicians.

BILL: mathematician, researcher and teacher

And so, a final section; a wrapping up of sorts. In texts of other genres, these are the pages of revelation; the heroine, against all odds, triumphs; the canny sleuth unmasks the scheming criminal. But this is neither a 'who-' nor a 'how-dunnit'. The perpetrators have been forthright from the outset. The mysteries they leave us with defy tidy statement and neat solution. Amongst them we might number: 'Why are the sorts of mathematical learning experiences described in the past chapters so rare?' and 'What are the factors which militate against this becoming more common?'

The rhythms and structure of this work have been such that I have been an 'after-the-fact' reflector for every section – a mathematical version of the dreaded 'action-replay commentator' on television sports programmes. While the number of times that I have regretted this limitation has been large – how exciting some of those classroom moments must have been – it is a constraint which has, until now, been tolerable. But at this point, a phrase from a recent book seems all too appropriate and I play mentally with the prospect of a different order of things.

The American writer, Erica Jong (1994), shared a pearl of generational advice in the early pages of her latest book, *Fear of Fifty*. Her father had been a vaudevillian in his youth and one bit of wisdom he distilled from that experience and passed on to his somewhat puzzled child was: 'never follow a dog act' (p. xix). Rena's and Eileen's sections preceding this one have been polished and powerful pieces of work – what Papa Jong would have recognised as competition of the worst canine sort. The primacy of pattern has, however, been set and my 'post-pooches' fate determined.

The acknowledgment of the talents of my collaborators perhaps makes this an appropriate place to confront what might be one of the less constructive, but probably not uncommon, reader responses to a book like this one. This is the categorisation of Eileen and Rena as, 'yes, but they are special', with its implied corollary, 'an ordinary teacher like myself, in an ordinary classroom with ordinary kids couldn't do all that stuff'.

This is not any easy position to refute, largely because so many of these perspectives are self-fulfilling. If you are convinced that you will not be able to do something, it is highly likely that you will find yourself unable to do it. Analogies with attempting to learn certain physical skills, such as swimming or skating, might be helpful here. At some point, usually associated with a situation characterised by interest, modelling, trust and experience, a learner overcomes anxieties and fears and passes to a new level of competence.

An encouraging recent trend in mathematics education research has been the emergence of naturalistic studies of classroom teachers struggling, openly and honestly, with the many demands of teaching (Romagnano, 1994; Schifter, 1996a, 1996b). When combined with a powerful intellectual framework, studies of this sort illuminate the current structurings and social and intellectual challenges of contemporary classrooms in very powerful ways (Davis, 1996). One message which is documented clearly in studies of this sort is that 'ordinariness' is a very difficult concept to capture in educational settings.

Children, in particular, defy this sort of categorisation. They are, often in dramatically different ways, resourceful and indefatigable, one-of-a-kind learning machines, albeit all too frequently, misguided, demanding and difficult ones. Taking the same approach it can be argued that there really are no 'ordinary' classrooms or teachers. The levels of complexity involved here are such that every instance is a unique case. So yes, Eileen and Rena are special, but in an important way this is true of all teachers.

The critical distinction to make is between their specialness in the sense of being unique individuals and being special in the sense of having a large number of personal characteristics and abilities which contribute to their effectiveness as teachers. There is no possibility of 'copying' in the first sense; cloning is, at least in this context, not an option. Copying in the second sense, while not easy, is feasible, and might well be seen as a good way to think of teacher education. What are the factors which contribute to the teaching effectiveness of these individuals and how might others come to emulate them? This echoes David Pimm's question from the preface: 'What is appropriable?'

Of the many characteristics and abilities which might be identified in the cases of Eileen and Rena, perhaps the most important is that of a prevailing sense of trust. At a fundamental level they trust themselves; they also trust their pupils. Once again there is an element of self-fulfillment and reciprocity here. Because they trust their pupils there is a natural tendency for the pupils to trust them. An atmosphere created by this sort of dynamic permits risk-taking of the sort we have seen paying such rich dividends.

A related insight which comes from knowing oneself well is the awareness that real knowledge and deep understanding do not happen quickly; as the fashionable abbreviation goes, 'TTT'. Things take time. So, of course, no teacher will be able to change patterns and behaviours radically in a short time and have immediate success doing 'all that stuff'. Some may make a few, carefully chosen changes as a small beginning and use them as the growing tip of what will become over time a set of substantially different ways of working with children in mathematics.

It is relatively easy to understand the concept of trust as it applies to individuals. There is, though, also a sense in which Rena and Eileen have exemplified in this work an important trust which is less frequently observed or commented on. This is a trust in the subject of mathematics. Because of this trust, they are less frightened of the 'unbeaten track'. Teachers lacking trust in this sense feel compelled to stay on the well-trodden, perhaps even polluted, paths of the so-called 'basics'. The traffic-jams and pot-holes on this particular highway are hazards to both the emotional and intellectual health of mathematics learners. It is with a more detailed consideration of a fundamental question related to this third sense of trust that I would like to end my remarks.

The central issue in the end, as I see it emerging, in differing ways, from the perspectives of all three of us, is: 'What is mathematics?'. For too long, educational discussions on themes such as 'How do children learn mathematics?' and 'What is the best way to teach mathematics?' have paid scant attention to the final word in the question. Mathematics has been taken for granted and, like anything which suffers this fate, has come to be seen as stale and lifeless.

Confusion and delusion

The current state of affairs concerning mathematics education can be characterised as that of confusion and delusion. Such confusion arises from the general public having an exceptionally fuzzy idea of just what mathematicians do. To the extent that lay people have conceptions about mathematics and mathematicians, these are often very negative. We have already noted the 'real-women-don't-do-maths' image with its 'Barbie-doll' spokesmannequin. Another negative public perception of mathematicians is that they are intellectually very clever, but socially inept and somewhat bizarre individuals.

Children's images of mathematicians have, for many years, been even less positive than their perceptions of scientists (Hudson, 1967). The scientist maintains a touch of romance, but the mathematician is seen as grey, boring and robotic. The view from literature is often extremely critical: Furinghetti (1993) cites a passage from Robert Musil's *The Man Without Qualities*.

> Mathematics has entered like a demon into all the applications of life ... mathematics is the origin of the perfidious reason that makes man master of the world and the slave of machines. The inner sterility, the monstrous mixture of rigour in minutiae and indifference to the whole, the desolate loneliness of man in a tangle of details, his anxiety, his wickedness, the fearful aridity of his heart, the thirst for money, the coldness and violence, that mark our times are ... only and simply consequences of the damage that logical and rigorous reasoning causes to the soul! ... Mathematics, mother of the exact sciences, grandmother of technology, was also the matrix of that spirit that later produced poison gas and bomber planes.
>
> (p. 35)

The French philosopher Simone Weil writes of the three monsters of the twentieth century: money, mechanisation and algebra. These last two critics cannot be dismissed lightly. Musil was an exceptionally well-educated individual with a strong background in engineering as well as philosophy. Weil, despite dying young, was a highly-regarded philosopher whose brother André would be considered by many knowledgeable observers to be one of the great contemporary mathematicians.

The deception or delusion component – these terms are perhaps too strong – can be seen as the responsibility of the mathematical research community who have, for the most part, done little to help develop a public understanding of the subject. Because of this, two levels of 'delusion' have evolved.

The first delusion arises from a view held by some members of the general public that maths is nothing but 'big sums'. This perception is reflected in questions at the school level of the sort: 'When are we ever going to use this stuff?', or in adult circles as: 'I have been successful in the real world and never had to use any algebra (or whatever) – hence, why are we still teaching it?' In the opening chapter, Rena stated that she 'didn't feel like a mathematician'. Nor is it surprising that she did not. There are certainly very few teachers in schools who think of themselves as mathematicians.

This is a major reason for the imbalance between compliant and creative activities in mathematics classes and a significant factor in the fundamental lack of authenticity in many classrooms. For the small percentage of students that go on to take one or more mathematics courses at the university level, the style of teaching is rarely invitational. The image of mathematicians which emerges is that of a small and isolated community who are not unhappy to be left alone. One of the few inside voices to make a public issue of this is Jerry King (1992).

> In the academy, many consequences follow from ... the perpetuation of the mystery of mathematics. One consequence, of enormous significance, is the great degree of freedom from external control and evaluation enjoyed by mathematicians. Non-mathematicians, both professors and administrators, feel illiterate and intimidated in the presence of mathematics and believe themselves incompetent to bring to bear on mathematicians standards they routinely apply to other colleagues.
>
> (pp. 222–3)

The second level of delusion – although 'misinterpretation' is perhaps a more accurate term – is more subtle. It comes from within the scientific and technical community in the form of the view that 'mathematics is the servant of science'. From this perspective, mathematics exists as a set of techniques which are, from time to time, quite useful in helping do work in the really interesting areas of human endeavour which have to do with physics, physiology, or engineering. How, why, when, or by whom these tools evolved is of no particular interest. The net effect of this is that mathematicians are under pressure from two directions. On the one side is a general public whose attitude toward the discipline is problematic. From the other side, the 'mathematics as a collection of techniques' camp is coming to see their calculator and computer toolboxes as almost all they need.

Until lately, this situation has been of little concern to most research mathematicians. In fact, as King suggests, there may well have been fairly widespread satisfaction with this state of affairs. As fiscal pressures have begun to be felt at all levels of society, there has, however, been increased awareness that this *laissez-faire* attitude may have been unwise. One example of this comes from the area of research funding. That part of the general public which is confused about the nature of mathematics includes almost all publicly-elected legislators. In their efforts to find suitable places to reduce spending, mathematics research funding has appeared to many as a highly suitable area.

A recent Canadian example would appear to be something of a classic of its type. A zealous and bellicose conservative backbencher announced with no small amount of self-satisfaction that he had uncovered the hitherto unsuspected scandal that the taxpayers' dollars had been funnelled toward research on 'Lie Theory'. While the more jaundiced among the electorate might think that this might be an area which politicians would be rather interested in promoting, our hero pledged himself to the eradication of this misappropriation of a part of the hard-pressed public purse. It is not recorded what his reaction was when he was informed that the research in question concerned itself with extensions of the work of the Scandinavian mathematician, Marius Sophus Lie (pronounced 'lee') to algebraic systems, fundamental to several fields of twentieth-century scientific research.

Our perspective up to this point has largely been local and inward-looking. We have noted and reflected on the interactions of individual children and teachers with a number of mathematical and aesthetic topics. The implications of this work for the larger educational debate are, however, quite significant. Let me try to illustrate this with two examples. The first comes from within the mathematics education community, and the second from a more general view of educational reform.

I noted in the first chapter that there are numerous similarities between the methods used by Rena and Eileen and the ideas outlined in the series of publications known as the American NCTM (National Council for Teachers of Mathematics) Standards. These documents (Curriculum and Evaluation, 1989; Professional Practice, 1991, and, Assessment, 1995) and their related implementation programmes constitute the most substantial and significant efforts at mathematics curriculum reform at the school level in the US for at least twenty-five years.

The resources, energy and imagination which have been dedicated to their development have been impressive and the overall project can legitimately be regarded as an exceptionally influential and successful exercise (Black and Atkin, 1996). I have no doubt that the individuals who constructed the Standards would be more than happy to endorse much of Rena and Eileen's work as excellent examples of their vision. In addition, this is an endorsement which Eileen and Rena would, in most ways, be happy to accept, knowing that their approaches are largely in agreement with the spirit of these initiatives.

There are, however, significant differences as well. Perhaps most important is that of underlying assumptions. The NCTM vision is still fundamentally a 'top-down' approach. It is rooted in ideas of power and control. On the one hand, this seems a natural, potent, and desirable basis for changing content and practice, particularly as it is expressed in the seductive language of 'empowerment'. On closer examination and deeper consideration, however, it seems that this perspective may well be risky and possibly deeply flawed. The idea of power is closely linked to the concepts of hierarchy and authority. The world of 'empowered/not-empowered' is inherently two-dimensional and is structurally similar to the 'right/wrong' polarity which has been the touchstone of mathematics education as long as public education has existed.

It seems possible that under the surface of the changed rhetoric the same abstract, decontextualised version of mathematics instruction will prevail, driven by exercises, competition and exams. The alternative which Rena and Eileen's work points to is mathematics emerging out of activities which have inherent meaning for the children, rather than mathematics for the sake of mathematics. At first glance, this may not seem to be a particularly significant distinction: potentially, however, it is of the utmost educational importance.

One of the umbrella organisations supporting the NCTM initiatives is the Mathematical Sciences Education Board (MSEB). A brochure which they publish (both on paper from the Annenberg/CPB Maths and Science Project[27] and on the World Wide Web[28]) is entitled: 'What should I look for in a maths classroom'. Although it is short, this document is worth close examination from a critical perspective, because it embodies, both in form and in content, many of the issues with which mathematics educators are struggling (Noddings, 1994).

Its very brevity identifies it as a product of the age of music videos and quick, hard sells:

> Mathematical thinking is an all-purpose tool. ... Mathematics is nourishment for 21st century minds. It is non-fattening and cholesterol free. It *can* be available in your local classrooms if you know what to ask for. Help your schools to serve up the best mathematics available.

Most of this punchy, post-modern document concerns itself, however, with responses to the question: 'How will I recognise a good mathematics classroom when I see it?' It is in these answers that a specific example of the significant difference between Eileen and Rena's approaches and those of main-line mathematics education reformers lies. Seven of the sixteen behaviours which observers are directed to look for are responses to the question: 'What are students doing?'; the remaining nine with the query: 'What are teachers doing?'

Most of these descriptions would fit the activities outlined in the earlier pages of this book exceptionally well. For example, students are: 'communicating mathematical ideas to one another through examples, demonstrations, models, drawings, and logical arguments'; 'not just practising a collection of isolated skills'; 'interacting with each other as well as working independently'. Teachers for their part are: 'working with other teachers to make connections between disciplines to show how maths is a part of other major subjects that students are studying'; 'bringing a variety of learning resources, including guest presenters, into the classroom in order to increase learning options for all students'; 'challenging students to think deeply'.

But Eileen and Rena have gone further, and have made their pupils their co-workers in a way which the MSEB's consumerist vision, cousin to Ronald MacDonald and Sesame Street, cannot even imagine. The plastic façade drops only for a moment, but it is enough to reveal that the Disneyesque fantasy will more likely be realised as a coercive sweatshop than as a creative *atelier*. Recommended teacher behaviour number two gives the game away. Our model teacher will be adept at: 'moving around the room to keep everyone engaged in productive work'.

A second 'check list' comes from a more recent and more general consideration of the potential and realities of public education, the collection of essays edited by William Ayers called *To Become a Teacher: Making a Difference in Children's Lives* (1995). In a society where bland, banal, corporatist propaganda has dominated much of educational discourse for at least a decade, Ayers's book comes as a blunt and bracing call to arms with more than a whiff of 1960s idealism.

In his concluding essay, 'Ten alternative classrooms', Ayers pulls few punches. Citing John Taylor Gatto, he points to:

> the real lessons of American schooling, things like hierarchy, and your place in it, indifference, emotional dependency, provisional self-esteem, and the need to submit to certified authority. ... Nothing of real importance is ever undertaken, nothing is ever connected to anything else, nothing is ever pursued to its deepest limits, nothing is ever finished, and nothing is ever done with investment and courage.
>
> (p. 215)

Ayers moves from this dismal picture to ten 'sketches of what could be done by teachers today' (p. 216). Ayers's sketches transcend subject matter.

Despite our tight subject focus in this work, it is interesting to note how many of his sketches sound as if he had built them from observations of Rena and Eileen's classroom. Classrooms could 'be lived in in the present tense', 'become workshops for inventors', 'honour diversity truly and fairly', 'begin with high expectations and standards for all', 'be places where adults tell the truth', 'become thoughtful places that honour the thinking and work of teacher and students' and 'be fair places where people make a difference'.

Ayers ends his paper with a statement about the types of teachers he sees as being capable of creating these sorts of classrooms. These are teachers who:

> conceive of teaching as fundamentally ethical, political, and intellectual work, the task of people willing to plunge in alongside their students and search for ways to nourish teaching as a creative act that, like all creative acts, is characterised by uncertainty, mystery, obstacle, and struggle.
>
> (p. 220)

Not a bad description of my friends Phillips and Upitis I think, given by a person who has never met them.

The message which comes from Rena and Eileen's work should be a reassuring one for educators like Ayers. It says that mathematics, often seen as the cutting edge of the approach they find so repugnant, in the hands of the right teachers, can be a potent force for the sort of education they dream of and struggle for. For when mathematicians talk among themselves, their passions are seldom tools and techniques: considerations of efficiency and applicability, virtually all that the general public gets to hear about, come later, if at all. Their talk too is of 'uncertainty, mystery, obstacle, and struggle' and of creativity and joy.

Here, for instance, is the view of William Thurston (1995), one of the world's great contemporary mathematicians:

> There is real joy in doing mathematics, in learning ways of thinking that explain and organise and simplify. One can feel this joy discovering new mathematics, rediscovering old mathematics, learning a way of thinking from a person or text, or finding a new way to explain, or to view an old mathematical structure.
>
> (p. 34)

Peter Hilton (1992), another distinguished mathematical thinker, writes in a similar vein:

> Our primary reason for doing mathematics is that it fascinates us. It stimulates both our intellectual curiosity and our aesthetic sensibilities. It poses deep, significant questions, whose answers, if we are fortunate to obtain any, provide an immediate spiritual reward, which, however soon, gives way to a new wave of curiosity, and a new set of questions.
>
> (p. 275)

The British mathematics educator, David Pimm (1995), also concludes his recent book entitled *Symbols and Meanings in School Mathematics* with a reconsideration of the nature of mathematics. He writes:

> What is mathematics about? It seems to me it is fundamentally about we human beings ourselves: our languaging and attentions, our wills and desires, and the astonishment that these can conjure. It becomes a place we invest with our dreams of precision, exactness and permanence. It is about

the structures of our attention in relation to our inner and outer experience, our inner and outer meanings, our inner and outer worlds.

(p. 191)

Dreams and fascination, joy and spiritual rewards, wills and desires; things close to the essence of being human and also to the discipline of mathematics. I am indebted to Rena and Eileen for their rich examples of the connections. It would, I think, behove all of us who consider ourselves to be mathematics educators to try to go and do likewise.

Notes

1 INTRODUCTION

1   My thanks to Ann Anderson, Department of Mathematics and Science Education, University of British Columbia, not only for the initial introduction, but for her continued support as the research project evolved.

2   Lorri Nielson, of Mount St Vincent University, first used this term to me in a telephone conversation some time ago – and it stuck.

3   See, for example, AAUW, 1992; Campbell, 1986; Ellis, 1986; Gilbert and Pomfret, 1991; Holmes, 1991; Lave, 1988, 1991; Linn and Hyde, 1989; Woods and Hammersley, 1993; Yeloushan, 1989.

2 TESSELLATIONS

4   I have since found out that the silk can be ironed *before* rinsing out the resist. This means the colours are brighter in the finished product.

5   See the article by Klawe (1994) for the origin of the naming scheme for the *Tetris* pieces given in Figure 2.15.

4 PAPER JEWELS

6   The world wide web site for this article is http://www.ccs.queensu.ca/pubs/news/v6n3/ccs.html

7   Home page reference is http://www.cs.ubc.ca/nest/egems/home.html

5 KALEIDOSCOPES AND COMPOSITION

8   A gallery showing is a method of getting all the pupils to see everyone else's work in as short a time as possible. Those sharing work leave their papers on their desk or work space. Everyone walks around on a previously determined route, and sees what is offered. The rule for comments is that if you cannot say anything complimentary, do not offer a comment.

9   I am indebted to Hugh Allen, a fellow musician and a former colleague, for many a conversation about music and mathematics.

10   http://xerxes.nas.edu/nap/online/mctcc/index.html

11   http://cwis.nyu.edu/pages/mathmol/more.html

12   http://www.tc.cornell.edu/er/sci93/dis22origami/dis22origami.html

13   http://www.chem.duke.edu/research/prisant/protein/protein.html

14 http://www.lassp.cornell.edu/lifshitz/quasicrystals.html
15 http://www.texas.net/escher/products/penpuz.html
16 http://http.cs.berkeley.edu/~bh/
17 http://www.texas.net/escher/contest/current.html
18 http://www.opentext.com:8080/
19 http://www.clbooks.com/nbb/knuth.html
20 http://www.mathpro.com/math/
21 http://www.eiu.edu/ac/busi/lum/makeit.html
22 http://sln.fi.edu/tfi/activity/math/math-2.html
23 http://www.ccs.queensu.ca/pubs/news/v6n3/ccs.html

6 CHILDREN AS MATHEMATICIANS

24 See Atwell, 1987; Calkins, 1986; Gentry, 1987; Graves, 1983; Mills and Clyde, 1990; Newman, 1985, 1990; Wells, 1986.
25 See Baker and Baker, 1990; Baker, Semple and Stead, 1990; Burns, 1975; Burns and Tank, 1988; Reys, Suydam, and Lindquist, 1995; Souvigney, 1994; Van de Walle, 1990; Whitin, Mills, and O'Keefe, 1990.
26 See Davis, 1996; Duckworth, 1987; Duckworth, Easley, Hawkins and Henriques, 1990; Hodgkin, 1985; Lave, 1988.
27 Annenberg/CPB Project, The Corporation for Public Broadcasting, 901 E. Street NW, Washington, DC 20004.
28 http://www.nas.edu/mseb/mseb.html

APPENDIX A
Time line of the school year

	SEPT	OCT	NOV	DEC	JAN	FEB	MAR	APR	MAY	JUNE
Grade 3 (Rena)	tessellations			codes	animation					
					composition					
Grade 4 (Eileen)	paper weaving and tessellations			line art and string art			symmetry		TEACHERS' STRIKE	
Grades 3 and 4 (Rena and Eileen)		tessellations				animation	jewellery		TEACHERS' STRIKE	kaleidoscope

References

AAUW (1992) *How Schools Shortchange Girls*, a report of the American Association of University Women Educational Foundation, Washington, DC, AAUW Educational Foundation.

Adams, C. C. (1994) *The Knot Book: An Elementary Introduction to the Mathematical Theory of Knots*, New York, NY, Freeman.

Ainley, J. (1988a) 'Playing games and real mathematics', in D. Pimm (ed.) *Mathematics, Teachers and Children*, Hodder and Stoughton, London, pp. 239–248.

Ainley, J. (1988b) 'Mathematical thinking in the primary curriculum', *Unit 9, ME234: Using Mathematical Thinking*, Milton Keynes, Open University.

Atwell, N. (1987) *In the Middle: Writing, Reading, and Learning with Adolescents*, Portsmouth, NH, Boyton-Cook.

Ayers, W. (ed.) (1995) *To Become a Teacher: Making a Difference in Children's Lives*, New York, NY, Teachers College Press.

Baker, A. and Baker, J. (1990) *Mathematics in Process*, Portsmouth, NH, Heinemann.

Baker, D., Semple, C. and Stead, T. (1990) *How Big is the Moon? Whole Maths in Action*, Portsmouth, NH, Heinemann.

Belenky, M., Clinchy, B., Goldberger, N. and Tarule, J. (1986) *Women's Ways of Knowing: the Development of Self, Voice, and Mind*, New York, NY, Basic Books.

Berlekamp, E., Conway, J. and Guy, R. (1982) *Winning Ways for Your Mathematical Plays*, London, Academic Press.

Berman, M. (1983) *The Reenchantment of the World*, New York, Bantam.

Bissex, G. (1980) *GNYS AT WRK: A Child Learns to Write and Read*, Cambridge, MA, Harvard University Press.

Black, P. and Atkin, J. M. (1996) *Changing the Subject: Innovations in Science, Mathematics and Technology Education*, London and New York, Routledge.

Briggs, J. (1992) *Fractals: the Patterns of Chaos*, New York, Simon and Schuster.

Bruner, J. S. (1966) *Toward a Theory of Instruction*, New York, NY, W.W. Norton.

Burns, M. (1975) *The 'I Hate Mathematics' Book*, Toronto, Little, Brown, and Co.

Burns, M. and Tank, B. (1988) *A Collection of Math Lessons from Grades 1 Through 3*, New York, NY, Math Solution Publications.

Calkins, L. McCormick (1986) *The Art of Writing*, Portsmouth, NH, Heinemann.

Campbell, P. (1986) 'What's a nice girl like you doing in math class?' *Phi Delta Kappa*, 67 (7), 516–520.

Carlton, J. (1994) 'Stay out of the laundry room, son, your mother is playing Tetris', *Wall Street Journal*, May 28, Section D, p. 1.

Carroll, L. (1879; 1976) *The Complete Works of Lewis Carroll*, New York, NY, Vintage Books.

Cohen, J. and Stewart, I. (1995) *The Collapse of Chaos: Discovering Simplicity in a Complex World*, New York, NY, Penguin.

Courant, R. and Robbins, H. (1941) *What is Mathematics? An Elementary Approach to Ideas and Methods*, London, Oxford University Press.

Cuban, L. (1986) *Teachers and Machines: the Classroom Use of Technology since 1920*, New York, NY, Teachers' College Press.

Davis, B. (1996) *Teaching Mathematics: Toward a Sound Alternative*, New York, NY, Garland.

Davis, R., Maher, C. and Noddings, N. (eds) (1990) *Constructivist Views on the Teaching and Learning of Mathematics*, Reston, VA, NCTM.

de Bono, E. (1971) *The Mechanism of Mind*, Harmondsworth, Middlesex, Penguin.

DeJean, J. and Upitis, R. (1995) 'Using CD-ROM books and paperbacks in a Grade 7/8 poetry unit', unpublished manuscript, Kingston, Ontario, Faculty of Education, Queen's University.

Diehn, G. and Krautwurst, T. (1992) *Nature Crafts for Kids*, New York, NY, Sterling Publishing Co., Inc.

Donaldson, M. (1978) *Children's Minds*, Glasgow, Fontana.

Dreyfus, H., Dreyfus, S. with Athanasiou, T. (1986) *Mind over Machine: The Power of Human Intuition and Expertise in the Era of the Computer*, New York, NY, Free Press.

Duckworth, E. (1987) *The Having of Wonderful Ideas and Other Essays on Teaching and Learning*, New York, NY, Teachers' College Press.

Duckworth, E., Easley, J., Hawkins, D. and Henriques, A. (1990) *Science Education: A Minds-on Approach for the Elementary Years*, Hillsdale, NJ, Lawrence Erlbaum.

Dyson, R. (1995) 'The treatment of media violence in Canada since publication of the Marsh Commission Report in 1977', unpublished doctoral dissertation, Toronto, Ontario, University of Toronto.

Edelson, E. (1992) 'Quasicrystals and superconductors: advances in condensed matter physics', in A. Greenwood (ed.) *Science at the Frontier, Vol. 1*, Washington, D.C., National Academy Press, pp. 233–54.

Ellis, D. (1986) 'Not "one of the boys"', *Crucible*, 17 (5), 22–3.

Ernst, B. (1985) *The Magic Mirror of M.C. Escher*, Diss, Norfolk, Tarquin.

Escher, M. (1974) *The World of M.C. Escher*, New York, NY, Abrams.

Franklin, U. (1990) *The Real World of Technology*, Montreal, CBC Enterprises.

Furinghetti, F. (1993) 'Images of mathematics outside the community of mathematicians: evidence and explanations', *For the Learning of Mathematics*, 13 (1), 33–8.

Gardner, M. (1975) 'On tessellating the plane with convex polygon tiles', *Scientific American*, July; reprinted as Chapter 13, 'Tiling with Convex Polygons', in M. Gardner, *Time Travel and Other Mathematical Bewilderments*, New York, NY, Freeman, 1988, pp. 163–76.

Gardner, M. (1989) *Penrose Tiles to Trapdoor Ciphers*, New York, NY, W.H. Freeman and Co.

Gardner, M. (1994) 'Word ladders: Lewis Carroll's doublets', *Math Horizons*, November, 18–19.

Gattegno, C. (1970) *What We Owe Children: The Subordination of Teaching to Learning*, New York, NY, Outerbridge and Dienstfrey.

Gentry, J. R. (1987) *Spel . . . is a Four-Letter Word*, Portsmouth, NH, Heinemann.

Gilbert, S. and Pomfret, A. (1991) *Gender Tracking in University Programs*, Ottawa, Government of Canada.

Gleick, J. (1987) *Chaos: Making a New Science*, New York, NY, Penguin.

Graves, D. (1983) *Writing: Teachers and Children at Work*, Portsmouth, NH, Heinemann.

Gruber, M. (1977) *The Essential Piaget*, London, Routledge.

Haines, T. L. (1993) 'Crocheted baby's blanket', unpublished manuscript, Vancouver, British Columbia, Department of Math and Science Education, University of British Columbia.

Hawkins, D. (1964) *The Language of Nature*, San Francisco, CA, Freeman.

Hawkins, D. (1974) *The Informed Vision: Essays on Learning and Human Nature*, New York, NY, Agathon.

Higginson, W. (1984) 'About that rose garden: remarks on Logo, learning, children and schools', *Proceedings of the 1984 National Logo Conference*, Cambridge, MA, MIT Media Laboratory, pp. 31–7.

Hilton, P. (1992) 'The joy of mathematics: A Mary P. Dolciani lecture', *College Mathematics Journal*, 23 (4), 274–81.

Hodgkin, R. (1985) *Playing and Exploring: Education Through the Discovery of Order*, London, Methuen.

Hoffman, P. (1988) *Archimedes' Revenge: the Joys and Perils of Mathematics*, New York, NY, Norton.

Holmes, N. C. (1991) 'The road less traveled by girls', *School Administrator*, 48 (10), 16–20.

Hudson, L. (1967) *Contrary Imaginations*, Harmondsworth, Middlesex, Penguin.

Inkpen, K., Upitis, R., Klawe, M., Hsu, D., Leroux, S., Lawry, J., Anderson, A., Ndunda, M. and Sedighian, K. (1994) 'We have never forgetful flowers in our garden: girls' responses to electronic games', *Journal of Computers in Mathematics and Science Teaching*, 13 (4), 383–403.

Jackson, P. (1992) *Untaught Lessons*, Chicago, IL, University of Chicago Press.

Jardine, D. (1995) 'The stubborn particulars of grace', in B. Horwood (ed.) *Experience and the Curriculum*, Dubuque, Iowa, Kendall/Hunt, pp. 261–75.

Jerome, J. (1989) *Stone Work: Reflections on Serious Play and Other Aspects of Country Life*, New York, NY, Penguin.

Jong, E. (1994) *Fear of Fifty: A Midlife Memoir*, New York, NY, Harper Collins.

Kappraff, J. (1991) *Connections: the Geometric Bridge Between Art and Science*, New York, NY, McGraw-Hill, Inc.

Kershner, R. B. (1968) 'On paving the plane', *American Mathematical Monthly*, 75, 839–44.

Kidder, T. (1985) *House*, Boston, MA, Houghton Mifflin.

King, J. (1992) *The Art of Mathematics*, New York, NY, Plenum Press.

Klawe, M. (1994) 'Bringing mathematical research to life in the schools', in C. Gaulin *et al.* (eds) *Proceedings of the 7th International Congress on Mathematical Education*, Québec, Laval University Press, pp. 27–45.

Kleinfeld, J. and Yerian, S. (1991) *Preparing Prospective Teachers to Develop the Mathematical and Scientific Abilities of Young Women: The Development of Teaching Cases*, unpublished manuscript Fairbanks, Alaska, Alaska University.

Knuth, D. (1968) *The Art of Computer Programming: Volume One: Fundamental Algorithms*, Reading, MA, Addison-Wesley.

Knuth, D. (1969) *The Art of Computer Programming: Volume Two: Semi-numerical Algorithms*, Reading, MA, Addison-Wesley.

Knuth, D. (1973) *The Art of Computer Programming: Volume Three: Sorting and Searching*, Reading, MA, Addison-Wesley.

Knuth, D. (1978) 'Lewis Carroll's Word, Ward, Ware, Dare, Dame, Game', *Games*, July–August.

Koch, C. and Upitis, R. (1996) 'Is equal computer time fair for girls? Potential

Internet inequities', *Proceedings of the 6th annual Conference of the Internet Society*, INET '96, Montréal, Québec.

Kreischer, L. (1971) *Symmography*, New York, NY, Crown Publishers.

Lakatos, I. (1976) *Proofs and Refutations: The Logic of Mathematical Discovery*, Cambridge, Cambridge University Press.

Langer, E. (1989) *Mindfulness*, Reading, MA, Addison-Wesley.

Lave, J. (1988) *Cognition in Practice: Mind, Mathematics, and Culture in Everyday Life*, Cambridge, MA, Cambridge University Press.

Lave, J. (1991) *Situated Learning: Legitimate Peripheral Participation*, Cambridge, Cambridge University Press.

Lightman, A. and Brawer, R. (1990) *Origins: The Lives and Worlds of Modern Cosmologists*, Cambridge, MA, Harvard University Press.

Linn, M. and Hyde, J. (1989) 'Gender, mathematics, and science', *Educational Researcher*, 18 (8), 17–27.

Manin, I. (1977) *A Course in Mathematical Logic*, London, Springer-Verlag.

Mayeroff, M. (1972) *On Caring*, New York, NY, Perennial Library.

Menninger, K. (1969) *Number Words and Number Symbols: A Cultural History of Numbers*, Cambridge, MA, MIT Press.

Mills, H. and Clyde, J. A. (1990) *Portraits of Whole Language Classrooms: Learning for All Ages*, Portsmouth, NH, Heinemann.

Nabokov, V. (1962) *Pale Fire*, London, Weidenfeld and Nicholson.

NCTM (1989) *Curriculum and Evaluation Standards for School Mathematics*, Reston, VA, National Council for Teachers of Mathematics.

NCTM (1991) *Professional Standards Practice for Teaching Mathematics*, Reston, VA, National Council for Teachers of Mathematics.

NCTM (1995) *Assessment Standards for School Mathematics*, Reston, VA, National Council for Teachers of Mathematics.

Negroponte, N. (1995) *Being Digital*, New York, NY, Knopf.

Newman, J. (1985) *Whole Language: Theory in Use*, Portsmouth, NH, Heinemann.

Newman, J. (1990) (ed.) *Finding Our Own Way: Teachers Exploring Their Assumptions*, Portsmouth, NH, Heinemann.

Noddings, N. (1994) 'Does everybody count? Reflections on reforms in school mathematics', *Journal of Mathematical Behavior*, 13, 89–104.

Opie, I. (1969) *Children's Games in Street and Playground: Chasing, Catching, Seeking, Hunting, Racing, Duelling, Exerting, Daring, ...*, Oxford, Clarendon Press.

Papert, S. (1980) *Mindstorms: Children, Computers, and Powerful Ideas*, New York, NY, Basic Books.

Papert, S. (1985) 'Computer criticism vs. technocentric thinking', *Logo 85 Theoretical Papers*, Cambridge, MA, MIT, pp. 53–67.

Papert, S. (1993) *The Children's Machine: Rethinking School in the Age of the Computer*, New York, NY, Basic Books.

Penrose, R. (1989) *The Emperor's New Mind: Concerning Computers, Minds and the Laws of Physics*, Oxford, Oxford University Press.

Peterson, I. (1990) *Islands of Truth: A Mathematical Mystery Cruise*, New York, NY, W. H. Freeman and Co.

Phillips, E. (1996) *This too is Math: Making Sense with a Pre-Schooler*, unpublished MA thesis, Vancouver, British Columbia, University of British Columbia.

Phillips, E. and Anderson, A. (1993) 'Developing mathematical power: a case study', *Early Child Development and Care*, 96, 135–46.

Piaget, J. (1952) *The Origins of Intelligence in Children*, New York, NY, International Universities Press.

Pimm, D. (1995) *Symbols and Meanings in School Mathematics*, London, Routledge.

Polya, G. (1957; 1971) *How to Solve It: A New Aspect of Mathematical Method*, Princeton, NJ, Princeton University Press.

Postman, N. (1992) *Technopoly: The Surrender of Culture to Technology*, New York, NY, Knopf.

Provenzo, E. (1991) *Video Kids: Making Sense of Nintendo*, Cambridge, MA, Harvard University Press.

Radecki, T. (1990) *TV and Other Forms of Violent Entertainment: A Cause of 50% of Real-Life Violence*, Champaign, IL, I-CAVE.

Reys, R. E., Suydam, M. N., and Lindquist, M. M. (1995) *Helping Children Learn Mathematics*, Boston, MA, Allyn and Bacon.

Romagnano, L. (1994) *Wrestling with Change: The Dilemmas of Teaching Real Mathematics*, Portsmouth, NH, Heinemann.

Rucker, R. (1982) *Infinity and the Mind: The Science and Philosophy of the Infinite*, Boston, MA, Birkhäuser.

Rucker, R. (1987) *Mind Tools: The Five Levels of Mathematical Reality*, Boston, MA, Houghton Mifflin.

Rucker, R. (1994) *Mathenauts: Tales of Mathematical Wonder*, New York, NY, Arbor House.

Sawyer, W. W. (1957) *Mathematician's Delight*, Harmondsworth, Middlesex, Penguin.

Sawyer, W. W. (1963) *Prelude to Mathematics*, Harmondsworth, Middlesex, Penguin.

Saxton, S. and Upitis, R. (1995) 'Game resisters, players, and creators: adolescents and computer games', unpublished manuscript, Kingston, Ontario, Faculty of Education, Queen's University.

Schattschneider D. (1981) 'In praise of amateurs', in D. Klarner (ed.) *The Mathematical Gardner*, Belmont, CA, Wadsworth, pp. 140–66.

Schattschneider D. and Walker, W. (1977) *M.C. Escher Kaleidocycles*, New York, NY, Ballantine Books.

Schifter, D. (ed.) (1996a) *What's Happening in Math Class? Volume 1. Envisioning New Practices Through Teacher Narratives*, New York, NY, Teachers College Press.

Schifter, D. (ed.) (1996b) *What's Happening in Math Class? Volume 2. Reconstructing Professional Identities*, New York, NY, Teachers College Press.

Senechal, M. (1994) 'Tilings, diffraction, and quasicrystals', *The Mathematical Journal*, 4 (2), 10–15.

Seymour, D. and Britton, J. (1989) *Introduction to Tessellations*, Palo Alto, CA, Dale Seymour Publications.

Singmaster, D. (1988) 'Mathematical games and recreations', in Hirst, A. and Hirst, K. (eds) *Proceedings of the Sixth International Congress on Mathematical Education*, Budapest, Hungary, ICMI Secretariat, Janos Bolyai Mathematical Society, pp. 361–4.

Sitomer, H. and Sitomer, M. (1970) *What is Symmetry?*, New York, NY, Thomas Y. Crowell and Co.

Smith, J. M. (1964) 'The limits of molecular evolution', in I. J. Good (ed.) *The Scientist Speculates*, London, Heinemann, pp. 252–6.

Souvigney, R. J. (1994) *Learning to Teach Mathematics*, Toronto, Maxwell Macmillan.

Stairs, A. (1994) 'Indigenous ways to go to school: exploring many visions', *Journal of Multilingual and Multicultural Development*, 15 (10), 63–76.

Stenmark, J., Thompson, V. and Cossey, R. (1986) *Family Math*, Berkeley, CA, Lawrence Hall of Science.

Stewart, I. (1995) *Nature's Numbers: The Unreal Reality of Mathematical Imagination*, New York, NY, Basic Books.

Supraner, R. (1981) *Stop and Look! Illusions*, Mahwah, NJ, Troll Associates.

Teeters, J. (1974) 'How to draw tessellations of the Escher type', *Mathematics Teacher*, 64, 307–10.

Thurston, W. (1995) 'On proof and progress in mathematics', *For the Learning of Mathematics*, 15 (1), 29–37.

Tomkins, C. (1994) 'The piano principle', *New Yorker*, August 22 and 29, 52–65.

Turkle, S. (1984) *The Second Self: Computers and the Human Spirit*, New York, NY, Simon and Schuster.

Turkle, S. (1995) *Life on the Screen: Identity in the Age of the Internet*, New York, NY, Simon and Schuster.

Upitis, R. (1990a) *This Too is Music*, Portsmouth, NH, Heinemann.

Upitis, R. (1990b) 'Children's invented notations of familiar and unfamiliar melodies', *Psychomusicology*, 9 (1), 89–106.

Upitis, R. (1990c) 'Math, music and computers: linking Bach preludes with algebraic functions', *Ontario Mathematics Gazette*, 29 (2), 29–36.

Upitis, R. (1992) *Can I Play You My Song? The Compositions and Invented Notations of Children*, Portsmouth, NH, Heinemann.

Upitis, R. (1995a) 'No strings attached: personalizing mathematics', in B. Horwood (ed.) *Experience and the Curriculum: Principles and Practice*, Dubuque, Iowa, Kendall/Hunt, pp. 235–60.

Upitis, R. (1995b) *Multimedia: Not for Everyone, Not for Everything*, http://www.ccs.queensu.ca/pubs/news/v6n3/ccs.html

Van de Walle, J. A. (1990) *Elementary School Mathematics: Teaching Developmentally*, White Plains, NY, Longman.

Walkerdine, V. (1981) 'The practice of reason', report of the Thomas Coram Research Institute, London, University of London.

Walter, M. (1971) *Annette*, London, André Deutsch.

Walter, M. (1975) *Another, Another, Another and More*, London, André Deutsch.

Walter, M. (1985) *The Mirror Puzzle Book*, Diss, Norfolk, Tarquin.

Watt, D. (1983) *Learning with Logo*, New York, NY, McGraw Hill.

Weizenbaum, J. (1976) *Computer Power and Human Reason: from Judgement to Calculation*, San Francisco, CA, Freeman.

Wells, G. (1986) *The Meaning Makers: Children Learning Language and Using Language to Learn*, Portsmouth, NH, Heinemann.

Whitin, D. J., Mills, H., and O'Keefe, T. (1990) *Living and Learning Mathematics*, Portsmouth, NH, Heinemann.

Williams, M. (1989) *The Velveteen Rabbit, or How Toys Become Real*, Philadelphia, PA, Running Press.

Winn, M. (1977) *The Plug-In Drug*, New York, NY, Viking Press.

Woods, P. and Hammersley, M. (eds) (1993) *Gender and Ethnicity in Schools*, New York, NY, Routledge.

Yeloushan, K. (1989) 'Social barriers hindering successful entry of females into technology-oriented fields', *Educational Technology*, 29 (11), 44–6.

Zuboff, S. (1988) *In the Age of the Smart Machine: The Future of Work and Power*, New York, NY, Basic Books.

SOFTWARE

Concertware, Great Wave Software, California.
Counting on Frank, Electronic Arts, California.
Logo, Logo Computer Systems Inc., Montréal, Québec.
Tesselmania!, MECC School Products.
Tetris, Spectrum Holobyte Inc.

Index